To
Mary Beth Rappe,
may she be an
Ambassador of Good Will
in the days ahead,
with best wishes,
Anne Guthrie

Hassain S. Farooqui (signature)

MADAME ABASSADOR

· MADAME
· AMBASSADOR

◈ THE LIFE OF VIJAYA LAKSHMI PANDIT

◈ ANNE GUTHRIE

Illustrated with photographs

Harcourt, Brace & World, Inc., New York

TO MY MOTHER

HOSSAIN S. FAROOQUI

CONTENTS

◆ 1
◆ A NEW LEADER ON THE
WORLD STAGE

At the high desk in the General Assembly Hall of the United Nations sat a small, beautiful, gray-haired woman, all alone. Madame Vijaya Lakshmi Pandit was presiding over the Eighth General Assembly of the United Nations.

Usually the Assembly President was flanked by the Secretary-General on her right, the Executive Assistant on her left. But at this particular moment, they had gone out for consultation. She was alone. In her hand, she held a gavel, the symbol of her office.

On the afternoon of September 15, 1953, Madame Pandit, lovely in a gray sari that matched her wavy hair, stepped out of her car at the delegates' entrance of the United Nations and entered the building. Graciously she greeted arriving delegates whom she knew, then stepped onto the escalator to the delegates' floor. As it carried her upward, she looked up and smiled at the people gathered above. Cameramen took shot after shot until she stepped off the escalator and friends hurried forward to greet her. Slowly she worked her way into the Assembly Hall and to the desk marked INDIA, her progress impeded by friends and well-wishers, photographers and newsmen, until a warning signal sent delegates and reporters to their seats and cameramen scurrying out of the hall.

The retiring president, Lester Pearson of Canada, called the Eighth General Assembly to order and asked the delegates and visitors to stand for a minute of silence for prayer or meditation. The minute passed. The delegates again seated and Mr. Pearson's speech of farewell delivered, the next item on the agenda was the election of the new president. The question was: who would be chosen. It was rumored that something unusual was about to happen. There was an atmosphere of anticipation in the great hall.

After the ballots had been distributed, the Executive Assistant called the roll of the member countries. The delegates—all men except the leader of the delegation from India—went forward and placed their ballots in the box at the foot of the podium. When the roll call was over, the votes were counted, the report was submitted, and the retiring president announced: "Madame Vijaya Lakshmi Pandit is elected President of the Eighth General Assembly of the United Nations."

Tumultuous applause broke out and continued as the Chief of Protocol escorted Madame Pandit down the aisle and up onto the podium. Many times in previous years, as leader of India's delegation, she had gone up the first few steps to the speakers' dais to address the Assembly. This time she did not turn. She went on. Spontaneously, delegates and the public rose to their feet as she mounted the steeper steps to the desk above, where three men stood to welcome her. Mr. Pearson seated her in the chair he so recently had occupied and then left to join his delegation.

When the hall was quiet, Vijaya Lakshmi Pandit, now Madame President, expressed her appreciation of the honor conferred on her, which, she told the General Assembly, she considered a tribute to her country and a recognition of the part women had played and might play in the cause of good will and understanding among nations. She assured the Assembly that the high traditions her distinguished predecessors had established would inspire and guide her through the days ahead. Very simply but very solemnly, she closed with a pledge to the delegates that she would use her best endeavors to help bring their work to "a fruitful conclusion."

Again there was applause. When it had subsided, Madame President called for the next item on the agenda. The eighth session of the General Assembly was at work under the leadership of a woman—an intelligent, experienced, beautiful woman of the East who had been a minister in her own country, an ambassador in other countries, and who, because of her love of country and of freedom, had three times been sent to prison by a government that now helped to elect her to the highest international position the countries of the world can offer, that of President of the General Assembly of the United Nations.

◈ 2

◈ CHILDHOOD OF SWARUP KUMARI NEHRU

August 18, 1900, was a stormy day in the city of Allahabad in the United Provinces of North India. The wind blew a terrific gale and the rain came down in torrents while in Anand Bhawan, the luxurious and spacious home of Motilal Nehru, a baby girl was born.

It had been a bad year. The rains did not come; the land was parched and dry; the crops failed. Famine spread through the villages and many people died. The money lenders grew richer; the peasants grew poorer. Then, the day of this baby's birth, the rains came. The earth absorbed the life-giving water, and again there was hope for those who tilled the soil.

At Anand Bhawan, the *ayah* or nurse told Swarup Rani Nehru, the fragile little mother, that since the baby had come with the rain, she had brought good fortune. It was a sign. All her life the Nehru daughter would bring good fortune.

Immediately, word was sent to the father, Motilal Nehru, then in England, that a daughter had been born. Back came a cable: "Call her Swarup Kumari for her mother."

The Nehrus, as most families in India at that time, lived under the "joint family" system, with all members of the family living under the same roof. A son, when he married, brought his wife to his father's home; a daughter went to the home of her husband. After the death of the father, the eldest son took his place as head of the household and was responsible for the family until the other members were able to support themselves or contribute to the joint income. The mother, who was deeply respected by all, looked after the house, her authority accepted and her judgment welcomed by her daughters-in-law. When the mother died, the wife of the eldest son assumed her responsibilities.

In the joint family, aunts and uncles were looked upon with the same affection and respect as children gave to their parents. Usually there were several cousins about the same age in the household, so boys and girls did not need to leave home to find playmates. Even a second or third cousin was thought of as a brother or sister and often referred to as such. They learned much from each other and had a solid background of home life, for there was a close relationship between the older and the younger generation.

Swarup Kumari's father, Motilal Nehru, was the youngest son of Ganga Dhar Nehru who had been *Kotwal* or Supreme High Commissioner of Police of Delhi, the capital of India. It was a much-coveted position. In 1857, however, at the time of the Sepoy Mutiny, when Indian troops rebelled against the British, the family lost everything, including old family records brought from Kashmir in the 1700's. Stories of the past, however, had been handed down through generations so the Nehrus knew something of their ancient Kashmiri ancestry.

The tradition was that Pundit Raj Kaul, called Pundit because of his knowledge of Persian and Sanskrit, was one of the scholars and men of learning for which Kashmir was famous. About 1716, the Mogul Emperor Farrukhsiar went to Kashmir for relief from the heat of Delhi. While there, he met or heard of Pundit Kaul.

The Emperor had great respect for men of letters, so after his return to Delhi, he invited Raj Kaul and his family to come to the capital and promised that he would be received with favor and given recognition as a scholar. The invitation was accepted; Raj Kaul left Kashmir and probably never saw it again. When he arrived in Delhi, he was given a plot of land with a house on it located near a canal. To identify the new family, people called them Kaul Nahar (the Kaul family on the canal). As time passed, people dropped the Kaul and eventually Nahar became Nehru, the family name famous all over India and known throughout the world.

All went well for Raj Kaul and his descendants, one of whom, Pundit Lakshmi Nehru, was a well-known lawyer connected with the East India Company, which controlled the trade between Britain and India. His son, Pundit Ganga Dhar Nehru, was the Kotwal. In his portrait, which hangs in Anand Bhawan, he appears to have been a very distinguished person with a red beard, blue eyes, and a fair skin. He has a curved sword across his knees, the symbol of his office.

After the mutiny when the family lost everything, the Nehrus went to Agra with other evacuees. One story remains of the journey there. As the party trudged down the road, they passed several British soldiers who noticed a very fair little girl with them. The mutiny was so recent that the soldiers were filled with distrust and suspicion. They surmised that here was an English child kidnaped by the Indian family. They ordered the party to stop and tried to take the child from them. In vain, the Nehrus explained that she belonged to them, but as no one spoke English, the soldiers did not understand them. The Nehrus were having a most difficult time when, fortunately, others of the party caught up with them. One man knew sufficient English to convince the soldiers that this was an Indian child who belonged where she was. Many years later Swarup Kumari Nehru was to know British police who did take her away as they had tried to take her little cousin in the long ago.

With the other evacuees, the Nehrus settled in Agra, where in
1861 Ganga Dhar Nehru died. Several months later his son Motilal was born. His coming was a great delight to the grief-stricken
family. It was an unusual coincidence that he was born on May
6, 1861, the same day that the famous Indian poet Rabindra-
nath Tagore was born in Calcutta.

Some years later, when an older son in the Nehru family was
appointed to the High Court in Allahabad, the family moved
there. Motilal was sent to Muir Central College but did not graduate, for he had too much fun and found too many opportunities
for escapades that were more exciting to him than books and
study. When he failed in his examinations, his family was dis-
couraged. The young man, however, knew what he wanted to do.
He was devoted to his brother Nand Lal, who had studied law by
himself and then taken the bar examinations. Motilal decided he
would do the same. Three months later, he took the examinations
and passed. Then he went on for a higher rank by taking the High
Court Vakil Examination, where he came out at the head of the
list and was awarded a gold medal.

For three years Motilal Nehru served as an apprentice in a district court in Cawnpore and earned a reputation as an industri-
ous, hard-working young lawyer. His apprenticeship over, he
started a regular law practice and later went to the Allahabad
High Court. As he had proved himself successful, winning many
cases, the family decided it was time for him to marry. They
found for him an exquisite young Kashmiri girl of a good family.
She was barely fifteen, tiny, dainty, and very beautiful with a fair
complexion, hazel eyes, and rich chestnut-brown hair. Her hands
and feet were small and perfectly shaped. Swarup Rani Nehru
made an exquisite but shy little bride.

It was a happy day for her and all the family when, on
November 14, 1889, a baby boy was born. They named him
Jawaharlal, which meant "a ruby jewel."

After the two older Nehru brothers had died, the responsibility for their wives and children, as well as for his own family, be-

came Motilal's. It meant a heavy financial load, but he was doing well, his law practice had grown, and his income had increased. He began to make plans for a house of his own. Consequently, when an excellent dwelling was offered for sale, located in a large compound, as the grounds around an Indian house are called, he bought it.

The palatial white villa had high turrets and many columns, which supported wide, open verandas around the house. In the center was an open paved courtyard. There was a charming little summerhouse, with a pile of rocks inside that made a miniature mountain. A statue of Shiva, the Hindu god known as "The Pre-server," stood on top of it. From his head water trickled down into a pool below and made the summerhouse cool and refresh-ing. Flowers, which flourished in the dampness, blossomed pro-fusely.

On one side of the grounds were craggy old trees and a garden filled with gay flowers. In the rear was a fruit orchard with mango, guava, lemon, and other fruit trees. Beyond the orchard, a forest sloped down toward the Ganges River in the distance. There were tennis courts and a swimming pool with electric lights strung around it, to make it possible to swim at night or sit beside the pool on hot evenings. At that time few houses in Allahabad had swimming pools, so the one at the Nehrus' was a novelty. The servants' quarters were in a separate building at the rear. In another section were the carriage houses and the stables, where the riding and carriage horses were kept. There were ponies and a riding ring for the children, and there were dogs—many dogs— for Mr. Nehru was fond of hunting. A high wall, with large wrought-iron gates at the front, enclosed the compound.

Inside, the house reflected the life of Motilal Nehru. It was a blending of East and West, for although he was a Brahman, in-deed a Kashmiri Brahman who is said to be "the Brahman of the Brahmans," Motilal was reared in the English tradition. He was an Indian intellectual who was brought up to admire the British and who was proud that India was a part of the mighty British

Empire. His home combined the best of both India and England.

The family part of the house, where Swarup played as a small child, was furnished as any high-caste Hindu home would be, with Indian and Kashmiri furnishings. It centered around the room where all the family gathered to talk, to read, or to eat. Here one usually sat on the white marble floor with rugs and cushions for comfort. In the hot season, these were replaced by cool matting. Food was usually served to each person on a *thali*, a large traylike plate often made of silver. Rice was piled up in the middle of the thali, around which was placed small bowls in which vegetables or other food were served. In India, people eat with their fingers, and food is thought to taste better when the metal of spoon or fork does not detract from the flavor of well-spiced food. Near the dining room there is always a place for family and guests to wash their hands immediately before and after a meal. Swarup's own room was of no special interest to her as she grew up; it was only a place to sleep. The common gathering room meant most to all of them, for it was here that things happened. It was the center of the life of the family.

Across the inner court of the house were rooms furnished with English or European divans and desks, tables and chairs. There were beautiful rugs, Venetian glass, Dresden china, paintings and sculpture. An English-trained butler looked after this section and served meals as correctly as any butler in London. Here Motilal Nehru entertained his overseas visitors and clients or his Indian friends who had studied or traveled abroad and who enjoyed English food occasionally. It was often a surprise to an English official, who expected an Indian home to be quite different from the homes to which he was accustomed, to be ushered into an elegant drawing room and later served an English meal at a well-appointed table in a delightful dining room, perhaps even more lavish than any to which he was accustomed in England.

In Mrs. Nehru's sitting room there were very wide divans, well-padded and covered with Oriental rugs, with long bolsters and many cushions on them. Here one could kick off sandals or shoes and curl up comfortably to talk or read, loaf or sleep. Mrs. Nehru spent most of her time in the Indian side of the house. Since she did not speak English, she felt strange when her husband's friends talked and joked in the unfamiliar language. However, when she joined them, she charmed them with her smile if not with words.

Motilal Nehru named his new home Anand Bhawan, which meant "The Abode of Happiness" or "A Home of Joy." He delighted in sharing it with friends. People were always coming and going, during the day for business, in the evenings to talk politics and world affairs with their genial host. All over India, Motilal Nehru was known for his joviality. Although he had a violent temper, he also had a great sense of humor, and his laugh was said to roll out like the waves of the sea and engulf everything and everyone. Consequently, while there was an intellectual and aristocratic atmosphere about Anand Bhawan, there was also gaiety and fun.

The tiny girl, Swarup, was the pet of the household. She was surrounded by every comfort and luxury. She was pampered, loved, and spoiled. Whatever she wanted was hers. As she toddled about the house or played on the veranda or in the garden, the family was at her command; servants stopped to play with her; friends admired her loveliness—her eyes, her curly hair, her smile. She was enchanting and full of laughter. She also was independent, with a will of her own. People often commented how much like her father she was. Although named Swarup for her mother, the family called her Nanhi, which meant "little daughter," the name used for the first girl born into a Kashmiri family.

In her early years Nanhi knew nothing but happiness. Anand Bhawan became a part of her and truly was to her "A Home of Joy." Years later she said, "Anand Bhawan! I love it. I love every stone of it. It is home."

When Swarup was almost five years old, Motilal Nehru took his wife and children to England. Jawaharlal, then fifteen, had only studied with tutors. Now his father decided a more formal education in an English school would be good for him.

They set sail in May, 1905, and arrived in England in time for the Derby, the famous horse race, which in 1718 had been instituted by the twelfth Earl of Derby. With thousands of other spectators, the Nehrus went to Epsom Downs, near London, for they all loved horses. Swarup was only two years old when she was first put on a horse either with her father or a groom. Later she was allowed to go around the riding ring on her own small pony, which was called Bijli or Lightning.

Very soon, Mr. Nehru found a vacancy for Jawaharlal at Harrow, the famous English boys' school. After he was settled there, the family went to the continent, where Swarup's fifth birthday was celebrated in Wiesbaden, Germany, one of the well-known watering places of Europe. To make it a happy occasion for his little daughter, Mr. Nehru entertained the children of one of the schools. The German papers reported it as a birthday party given by "a friend of children, from India." While the Nehrus were in Germany, Swarup was invited to a party given for children by Kaiser Wilhelm II. Here the small guest from India was singled out as one of those to be presented to the Kaiser.

Before they left England to return home, Motilal Nehru made another decision. Swarup was growing fast; already she was reading books in Hindi and English. Her father knew she needed someone to guide and direct her. Also he wanted her to speak English without an accent, so it seemed wise for her to have an English governess. Mr. Nehru consulted friends, and Miss Cecilia Hooper was suggested. She was a well-qualified young woman of twenty-six with an excellent family background. An interview was arranged, and in his usual decisive fashion, after talking with her for only twenty minutes, Mr. Nehru offered her the post. She appreciated his directness and accepted for a year. He insisted it must be for at least a two-year period, since the journey to India

was a long one. Miss Hooper declared she would come for one
year or not at all. He recognized that she was a young woman
with a mind of her own and liked her for it. He knew that
Swarup's mother was seldom firm with her and that he himself
often spoiled her. Miss Hooper, he believed, would look after his
young daughter well, with discipline but also with kindness. He
accepted her terms. Cecilia Hooper came for one year and stayed
twelve.

◆ 3
◆ GROWING UP

Miss Hooper quickly adapted herself to the life at Anand Bhawan. She learned to enjoy Indian food, to appreciate Indian customs, and to speak Hindustani, a combination of Hindi and Urdu
used in North India. Cecilia Hooper became one of the Nehru
family, admired and respected by all. The children grew to love
her, for while she was exacting, efficient, and insisted on discipline, she was also affectionate. She organized games for them,
taught them songs, and gave them candy on special occasions.

The routine that Miss Hooper established for Swarup was a
new experience for the five-year-old child, but she soon grew accustomed to it. Miss Hooper was strict and expected to be
obeyed. When she said a task was to be done, there was no ques-
tioning, no begging off, no delay. Her young charge soon realized, however, that while Miss Hooper was firm, she was always
fair.

The family called Swarup by her Kashmiri name, Nanhi, but
it had no meaning for her governess, so Miss Hooper shortened
it to Nan. At that time, there was much British influence in the
wealthy and intellectual circles of India, and it was the vogue to

use English names, so Swarup's friends adopted the new name and the little girl grew up known to many as Nan Nehru.

The program that her governess planned for Nan was much the same as that of an English schoolgirl. She was up early for a cold shower, followed usually by a short ride around the ring on her pony. Breakfast over, lessons followed, either with Miss Hooper or with one of the tutors. If Nan liked the subject, she learned quickly; if it did not interest her, she would pay little attention and dream about something else. History and geography she enjoyed, but arithmetic she disliked. Maps were a delight to her, but as she pored over them, neither she nor her tutor dreamed that in later years she would be visiting the various continents that she traced out with her chubby little finger.

Most of the time, Nan and her governess had their meals together and ate English food. Their cook also planned the meals when there were European guests. After lunch Miss Hooper insisted on a nap; then in the late afternoon, when it was cooler, there were games or a drive, at times in Mrs. Nehru's smart brougham, a four-wheeled closed carriage drawn by a pair of beautiful horses. Often they would drive along the river, which the tutor said should not be called Ganges but "Ganga," the Sanskrit word for "Goer" or "The Swift One."

Much of the time, Nan lived in a make-believe world. Since there was no one her own age to play with, she was often alone, so she played "make-believe," perhaps draping herself in a *sari* of her mother's and climbing into a high-backed chair to be some famous personage. Nan knew little about the world outside of her own family, except that her brother was studying in England. She wore English dresses, which came regularly twice a year from Liberty's in London, one of the well-known shops. Her everyday dresses were made by Mohammed Hussein, a *darzi* or tailor, who came to the house regularly and sat cross-legged on the back veranda to do the family sewing, in a shady corner if it was hot, in the sun if the day was cool. Nan loved to watch him and to hear the soft buzzing sound of his small hand-powered sewing machine.

Nan was seven when a baby sister came to add to the happiness of the Nehru family. For several weeks, the tiny sister had no name. Jawaharlal, in England, had been asked to suggest one. Finally word came that since he did not know whether he was to name a sister or a brother, he had chosen "Krishna," which was appropriate for either one. He did not actually see his small sister until she was five years old. After the birth of this child, Mrs. Nehru was very ill. Gradually her health improved, but for years she was not strong. For Nan the days were much the same, however, as most of her time was spent with Miss Hooper.

Nan's chief joy was her father. It was always fun to be with him. Her mother lacked a sense of humor and often failed to understand their jokes. When this happened, Nan and her father would laugh even more because Mrs. Nehru looked so puzzled and so serious. Occasionally Motilal Nehru's temper would flair up, but it went as quickly as it came. Nan was sure there was no one more wonderful than he was.

Mr. Nehru spent much of his time in his office or in one of his libraries, for in addition to the general library where Nan spent many hours, he had a special law library. Nan loved the library, for it carried her all over the world. She would curl up in a chair, hide behind a book, and go to far places. Her aunt told her always to remember that within the covers of a book, there is knowledge. She must treat it as she would treat age, with respect. If she was careless with a book, which was very seldom, her mother would say to her, "These careless Western ways have no place in our lives," for anything Mrs. Nehru did not like or did not approve of was labeled "Western."

Nan learned what was expected of a well-brought-up Indian child, learned without thinking about it, from adults or from the older children. It was important to be friendly, to be thorough in all she did, and in every situation to do what was considered correct. She knew that she always must stand when an older person entered the room, no matter what she was doing or how interesting the book might be that she was reading. Some of her friends leaned over and touched the feet of an older person when greeting them, but Nan did not do this as it was not a Kashmiri custom. The younger members of the family realized that in later years it would be their responsibility to care for the older members. Thus, in part, they would repay the debt they owed for the care given them when they were children. This would not be considered an obligation but a privilege, since, when young, they had been looked after with love and affection.

Girls were expected to do things well so that, when they married, they could manage their husbands' homes. Both for the sake of their husbands and for the reputation of their own families, they must be skillful. Always in the background was the thought of the family: one would never do anything that would in any way disgrace its name. So Nan was taught to cook and sew and do the things that would be expected of every Indian girl after she was married. This was not difficult, for she loved cooking and delighted in watching the cook as he made the dishes she especially liked.

As she grew up, Nan had one disappointment. The mark of a beautiful young woman was long hair. Her mother's hair fell below her knees, while Nan's barely came to her shoulders. No matter how much coconut oil the ayah rubbed into it, it would not grow long. It was thick and curly, but short. Also, in her early teens she was fat, and her cousins called her "Fatty," which she hated. Often she wished she were a boy. The cousins she played with were all boys, but since they were older than she was, they did not like to include her in their games. Nan also enjoyed boys' books more than those written for girls. She read many English books and came to know Dickens, Thackeray, Shakespeare. Historical novels she especially liked, but it was maps that were to her the "high road to romance and adventure."

When Miss Hooper took Nan to a dancing class with British and European children, she was thrilled. Not even riding was such a delight. But when the family discovered how infatuated she was with dancing, the lessons were stopped. No nice Indian girl, her mother felt, would let a boy whirl her around as she saw the English boys do.

It was an exciting day for all the family and, indeed, for the city of Allahabad when the Nehru motorcar arrived. It was the first automobile in the city. Mr. Nehru showed off his Model-T Ford with pride and informed his friends it would go twenty miles an hour. Drivers of the bullock carts and the *tongas*, the two-wheeled horse-drawn carts, were terrified when Mr. Nehru passed them on the road. They were certain the horseless carriage was the invention of an evil spirit. Mr. Nehru kept his horses, nonetheless, and Mrs. Nehru preferred her carriage to the motorcar.

On Sunday mornings, Nan went with Miss Hooper to Holy Trinity, the little English church across the road from Anand Bhawan. Nan sat very primly beside Miss Hooper in her pew. While she did not understand the service, she liked the singing, especially at the Easter and the Christmas services. Often at an early hour when the air was fresh and the world just beginning to awaken, her mother went to a small Hindu shrine. It was built on a spot where the ancient hero Rama had stopped on his return from his long absence. For over two thousand years, a temple had stood there. When one decayed, another was built by some devout person. When Nan went with her mother, she loved the sound of the temple bells. If the wind blew or there was a soft breeze, they tinkled in a pleasing fashion.

On special occasions, Mrs. Nehru would send a basket of flowers from her garden to the vicar's wife, to help decorate Holy Trinity; and when the fruit ripened in the orchard, a big basketful would be sent across to the vicar's house.

Nan's father had little interest in religion and considered himself an agnostic. But even though he was a skeptic, he did feel that all religions should be respected. He said that he left worship to the women of the family, so he approved of Nan's going to church with Miss Hooper and to the temple with her mother. The tinkle of the temple bells and the peal of the church chimes came to blend into a harmony for Nan.

When studies were over, Nan frequently went to the room of Bibi Amma, her mother's sister, who lived with them. This aunt had been married very young and was still a child when her husband died. She adored her younger sister and was devoted to her nieces and nephews; she told them stories from her inexhaustible store of folklore and read aloud to them selections from the "Bhagavad Gita," the longest poem ever written. The poem dates from sometime between the fifth and the second centuries B.C. As Nan grew older, she often read the "Gita" and the epic poem "Ramayana."

There were many holidays, some Hindu, others Moslem. Christmas was also a holiday. The Nehrus celebrated them all. For days before a festival, the house was decorated and the cook made the dishes or sweets appropriate to each occasion. On the day that began the Kashmiri calendar, the children were awakened with "Naoroz Mubarack," which meant Happy New Year. Although celebrated only by the Kashmiris, friends always came to Anand Bhawan to greet the Nehrus and to eat the delicious Kashmiri sweets.

A favorite celebration was Dewali. In the morning, trays of fruits and sweets were sent to friends and equally lovely trays came in return. The day began for Nan when she quietly went to the room of Bibi Amma to put a special sweet and the most perfect fruit that she could find on the shining silver thali placed under a picture of Lakshmi, the Goddess of Fortune, who sat on a pink lotus blossom. On the thali would be rice, flowers, and sweets. Nan would arrange her gifts with care, for she always liked things to be orderly and artistic. In the evening as it grew dark,

tiny lamps, which had been placed in rows on ledges and window sills, along the flat roof and around the turrets of the house,
were lighted. Anand Bhawan turned into a glittering palace out-
lined with stars. All the houses in Allahabad were illuminated.
Even those of the poorest people had for Dewali a few rough pot-
tery lamps, with string wicks burning in castor oil.

Allahabad is one of the famous old cities of India. Originally
it was called Prayag, and in ancient days was known as "a meeting place for men and women who placed spirituality far above
things of the world." It was Akbar, the wisest and greatest of the
Mogul rulers of India, who in the early 1600's gave Prayag the
name of Ilahabas, "The Abode of God," which later became Allahabad. Here the sacred rivers, the Ganges and the Jumna, meet.
The two streams are clearly distinguishable by their color—the
lighter stream of the Ganges mingling with the blue water of the
Jumna. A stanza from an ancient poem describes the conflu-
ence of the rivers as "a string of pearls interspersed with
sapphires."

Each year in December or January, there is a Magh Mela, a festival when thousands of people come to bathe at this sacred spot,
for through the centuries it has been a Hindu belief that by bathing in the water of the sacred rivers, all the pollution of sin is
washed away. Every twelve years this ceremony becomes the
Kumbh Mela, an enormous festival, with hundreds of thousands
of pilgrims and visitors coming from Cape Comorin to Kashmir,
from Assam to Sind. It is a spectacular occasion that binds all
Hindu India together, for pilgrimages to holy places make devout
Hindus feel that they are essentially one, though varying in many
other respects.

The Nehru home was located on a rise of ground that was famous as the place where the great hero Rama, after fourteen years
of exile, met his stepbrother Bharata. Rama had been sent away
by his stepmother, who wanted her own son to be heir to the
throne. Bharata was not happy about this and kept his brother's
slippers on the throne during the years of exile, to show that the

throne belonged to Rama. Everyone knew the story of the adventures of Rama and his joyous reunion with Bharata as told in
the epic poem, "Ramayana," written about 200 B.C., so people
often came to the Nehrus' compound to see the sacred spot.

The Bharadwaja Ashram, or "The Hermitage," was not far from
Anand Bhawan. Here Rama and Bharata were entertained when
they halted on their journey. Nearby was still another place of
pilgrimage because in ancient days there had been a university
there. Today the University of Allahabad and other centers of
learning are not far away.

Historic interest brought throngs of people past Anand
Bhawan and, if the gates were open, into the grounds. They also
were curious to see the home of Motilal Nehru, whose fame as a
lawyer was spreading over India. Although Mr. Nehru did not accept criminal cases, he was kept more than busy with civil ones.
He became so renowned that it was rumored one must pay a
thousand rupees a minute for his services. Whether or not this
was true, his fees were large and he was able to do more and
more to improve and beautify Anand Bhawan.

In this setting Swarup Kumari Nehru grew up. Her youthful
days were happy, carefree, and filled with many activities, among
which reading was always a favorite. As she grew older, she, like
many girls, had her heroines. One was of the present, a family
friend, Mrs. Sarojini Naidu, a politician and a poet with a most
delightful sense of humor. In 1917, she led a delegation of
women to present a memorandum to the British Secretary of
State demanding votes for women, as well as better educational
and health facilities. Later she was elected president of the Indian
National Congress, a political party. Nan's other very special hero-
ine, one of the recent past, was Rani Lakshmibai of Jhansi, a girl
of twenty who died fighting with the Indian soldiers against the
British soldiers in the Sepoy Mutiny of 1857. An English general
said of her that she was "the best and bravest" of the rebel leaders.

Since Nan Nehru was only fourteen when World War I broke out in Europe, it did not concern her very much, except that she knew Miss Hooper was worried as she read letters from home and from her friends in England.

In 1916, Nan's brother, Jawaharlal, who had worked in his father's law office since his return from Cambridge and the London law courts, was to be married. Nine-year-old Krishna could hardly contain her delight at the thought of a wedding. For Nan, now sixteen, it was also an exciting occasion.

Motilal Nehru was very happy about the marriage. He had seen Kamala Kaul at a wedding reception and been struck by her loveliness. She was tall and slim, with natural poise and the classic features of her Kashmiri ancestors. Mr. Nehru felt she would make a good wife for his son. There were few more eligible young men in India than Jawaharlal Nehru, well-educated, handsome, and of a distinguished family. Kamala's father, a Kashmiri Brahman, was a prosperous businessman in Delhi.

Since Kamala was only seventeen and her background was the traditional Hindu one, her contacts with Western ways were limited. She was gay and warm-hearted, frank and loyal with her friends, but with strangers Kamala was shy and reserved, almost frigid. Mr. Nehru realized this would be a handicap when she came to live in the cosmopolitan Nehru home, more so because Nan, only a year younger than Kamala, had been brought up in this cosmopolitan atmosphere and was outgoing and at ease with everyone. Consequently, Motilal Nehru made a most unusual suggestion, which Kamala's family eventually agreed to. She was to come for a few months to visit her aunt who lived in Allahabad and so become acquainted with her future home. Since Mr. Nehru had selected Kamala, he was determined she should be equal to the place she would have in the Nehru family. As the wife of his only son, she would be the hostess whenever his own wife was not well. As Kamala's English was limited, it was also agreed that Miss Hooper would help her. So she came to her aunt's home, and she and the Nehrus had an opportunity to know each other. Even so, she saw little of Jawaharlal, was never alone with him, and always was especially shy when he was present.

The horoscopes revealed that an appropriate date for the wedding, which would take place at the home of the bride in Delhi, was "Vasanta Panchami." This February day heralds the coming of spring and is the day when students garland their books and wear yellow in honor of Saraswati, the Goddess of Learning.

A week before the wedding date, the Nehru party of more than a hundred relatives, friends, and invited guests left Allahabad on a beautifully decorated special train. All along the way, people lined the roads and the station platforms to watch it go by. Hundreds of other guests, from all over India, joined them in Delhi. They proved to be too many for the houses Mr. Nehru had rented for the party, so tents were put up in the gardens, and the colorful colony was known as "The Nehru Wedding Camp." Festivities went on for ten days, and the wedding was a regal affair. Everyone admired the handsome groom and said they had seldom seen as lovely a bride as Kamala. People also commented on the Nehru daughter. The extra pounds had disappeared, and she had become an exceedingly attractive young woman. Friends began to wonder who the fortunate man would be who would win Swarup Kumari Nehru.

The wedding celebration over, the Nehru party returned to Allahabad, where Kamala and Jawaharlal settled into the new quarters that had been added for them at Anand Bhawan.

In India, when the hot season approaches and the sun begins to beat down in cruel fashion, all who can afford to do so leave their homes on the plains and go to the mountains, to the "hill stations." These towns are either tucked away in a cool mountain valley, situated on a high plateau, or set precariously on a mountainside. Many can be reached only by a trail or a path. Travelers must leave car or bus at the end of the road and walk or ride horseback, be pulled in a ricksha or carried in a *dandy* (a reclining chair carried on the shoulders of four men) to reach their destination. All of these hill stations are from five to ten thousand feet above sea level, where the days are usually cool and the nights cold. Here the fortunate few forget the burning heat on the plains below, where most of India's millions work or struggle to exist, all seasons alike to them.

The Nehru family was among those who were able to leave Allahabad for the hot months and stay away until the monsoon season came and the rain poured down to cool the earth. Occasionally they went to Simla, where the government spent six months of the year to escape the intense heat of Delhi. More often they took a house in Mussoorie or Naini Tal in their own province, a shorter distance to travel. The Nehrus planned sometime to go to Kashmir to live in a house on the land or in a houseboat on a lake. Of all the beautiful and picturesque vacation spots in the world, Kashmir is one of the loveliest, but it was a long and tiring journey from Allahabad.

Although the Nehrus had never been to the valley, it was of special interest for them because they were Kashmiri Brahmans. Even though the family records had been destroyed in Delhi in the Mutiny of 1857, they knew that for years, perhaps for centuries, the family, although called by another name, had lived in Kashmir surrounded by the lofty Himalaya Mountains, whose melting snows formed the great livers of India—the Indus, the Brahmaputra, and the Ganges. Here lakes nestled in high gorges or spread their blue waters in the valley below. Man-made canals linked the rivers and the lakes together. Great chinar trees, whose branches spread out like a canopy, provided shade. Those who lived there loved the valley intensely, although life was not easy, for there was little good land, and the winters were long and bitterly cold.

Kashmir was often called "a house of many stories," for it climbed up the sides of the mountains. It was shaped like a scimitar, its edge facing south, with the Himalayas piled up along its

frontier for fifteen hundred miles. At each end, lesser mountain
ranges turned southward, like arms outstretched to protect India
from east and west. China built her Great Wall; nature gave India
hers. Because of it, India was considered a subcontinent. There
was only one crack in this mountain wall, the famous Khyber
Pass on the main trade route from Kabul, Afghanistan, to Peshawar, India (now Pakistan). For centuries through this pass
camel caravans came loaded with goods from the north to sell
and returned with merchandise from India.

Beauty enriched the lives of the Kashmiris, no matter how poor
they were. This beauty they transferred to the things they made.
Shawls were woven from the soft fluffy "underneath wool" of the
goats, which became so famous that women the world over longed
for a Kashmiri shawl, especially one fine enough to be drawn
through the circle of a wedding ring. The wood of the forests was
carved into beautiful tables, trays, chairs, and many household
articles. Skilled workmen made papier-mâché boxes, an art
brought from Persia. These they decorated by painting on them
delicate designs or the flowers and birds of Kashmir. Silk was
woven, silver engraved; table covers were embroidered, rugs made
—all with an instinctive feeling for beauty.

Because of their ancestral roots in Kashmir, the Nehrus' holiday in 1916 had special significance for them. Mr. Nehru had
secured a camp in the Vale of Kashmir for the hot season. With
several friends, the family left Allahabad by train for Lahore. Here
they changed to the Frontier Express, which twice a week went
north to Peshawar, the most northern city of India, near the
Khyber Pass. The family, however, alighted at Rawalapindi to
continue the journey into the valley by motorcar. For two days,
with a pause in a hotel at night, the cavalcade of autos went up
and down the winding roads, climbing higher and higher into the
great Himalayas. In bygone days, to escape the heat of Delhi, the
Mogul rulers had gone over these same roads on elephants. Rest
stops were cut out of the mountainsides where they could dis-

mount, relax in the shade, drink the clear, cool mountain water, and eat their refreshments before continuing their leisurely journey. Overnight shelters were distanced as far apart as an elephant could walk in a day.

As the road wound up, then down, then up again, the vistas were breath-taking. On the second afternoon, as the cars went around a bend, suddenly, far below, could be seen, spread out like a green velvet carpet, the Vale of Kashmir. It stretched on and on until it was lost at the foot of the mountains that cupped it in. As the road zigzagged down into the valley, the shadows cast by the mountains were left behind until the cars reached the long, straight road that leads across the valley to Srinagar, the capital of Kashmir. Here it was again shady, for the Moguls had had poplar trees planted to turn the road into a tree-lined avenue. Down this road the party drove. The camp was near, their journey almost over. The Nehrus for the first time were in the land of their ancestors.

After the usual bargaining, arrangements were made for coolies to carry the baggage to the camp, where the family settled in for the season. For Nan and Krishna, it was not all holiday. Miss Hooper arranged their schedule, but when lessons were over, there might be visits to the shops to see the art work or picturesque *shakaras* were ordered for trips on the lakes and the canals. These boats were paddled by four or five men, who sat behind the high, comfortable padded seat, where occupants could relax with feet stretched out on cushions. Lunch baskets were packed if the outing was to Dal Lake to see the floating gardens of lotus blossoms, or to Nasim Bagh, the Garden of Breezes, where they picnicked under the trees. Nishat Bagh was a favorite spot for all visitors to Kashmir. Here the water of fountains splashed down from terrace to terrace, while in the distance the rugged Himalaya Mountains rose like a magnificent backdrop.

After a short time, with his cousins and a few friends, Jawaharlal Nehru left the camp for a couple of weeks to go up the

Ladakh Road and wander among the mountains. He had tramped and climbed in Switzerland and Norway but never in India. The party returned with tales of adventure, including Jawaharlal's fall into an icy crevice from which it had been difficult to extricate him.

Nan also had an exciting and unique experience that summer. It happened one sunny afternoon when the family sat by the creek that ran through the campgrounds. Nan had stretched out on the grass of a little island that divided the stream. Her chin was cupped in her hands, as, propped on her elbows, she read a book open in front of her. She was lost in her story when suddenly she heard her father's voice. His words came across to her almost in a whisper, yet distinct and positive, ordering her to lie absolutely still and not to move.

Across the stream the family watched, horrified, as a huge cobra, weaving its way through the grass, came so close to Nan that it almost touched her, its head near her head, which was still cupped in her hands. The great snake stopped, lifted its hood into the air, then, with a quick motion, thrust it out over Nan's head. Here it swayed slowly as the hand of a priest might move over a child in blessing.

The family watched. No one uttered a sound. Terror yet wonder gripped them. Then the cobra's hood relaxed, its head was lowered to the ground, and the cobra glided away and was gone.

In the late afternoon, a holy man, a mendicant, appeared at the gate and said he had come to tell the family that what had happened was significant for them, especially for the daughter. The cobra only spread its hood over one whom the gods would favor. He added, however, that as he looked into the future, he saw this daughter rise to great heights and achieve fame, but he saw suffering and unhappiness as well.

The hot season near the end, the Nehrus left the valley as Raj Kaul had left it long before. A few days later they arrived in Allahabad and drove through the gates of Anand Bhawan. Their roots were in Kashmir, but Allahabad was home.

The year 1917 held important events for the Nehrus. The first
was a surprise. Miss Hooper, in her twelve years at Anand Bhawan, had become so much a part of the family that they assumed
she would stay with them always. One day, to their astonishment,
she told them that she had met an Englishman who had asked
her to marry him. She had accepted and would like to do so as
soon as possible. As Miss Hooper's family was all in England,
Pundit Nehru gave the bride away. Nan and Krishna were brides-
maids at the wedding in the church across the road.

The family decided that, since Nan was now seventeen, a governess was not necessary and she might help Krishna with her
lessons until a new governess for the younger sister could be
found.

Another event of great importance occurred on November 19,
1917. Jawaharlal and Kamala's baby girl, Indira, was born. The
arrival of the first grandchild was celebrated by the Nehru family
in appropriate fashion. There was, however, a sad note in the
days that followed, for Kamala began to show symptoms of the
disease that was to cause years of suffering for her and years of
anxiety for her husband.

Shortly after Indira's birth, Motilal Nehru again demonstrated
what an unusual person he was by doing something contrary to
custom. He decided to build a separate house across the compound from Anand Bhawan for his son, in spite of the fact that
they had always lived under the accepted joint family system.
The home was to be a large two-story one, of the type of many
Bombay houses, with wide verandas both above and below.
Mr. Nehru worked on the plans for the house with whole-hearted
enthusiasm.

❖ 4

❖ GANDHI AND THE NEHRUS

Nan Nehru in her early teens had little concern for politics, but she could not avoid hearing the lengthy discussions and frequently heated arguments between her father and her brother about political questions and about a man named Mohandas Gandhi, who had returned from South Africa when she was fourteen. She learned that he came from Gujarat, where his father had been a *dewan* as her grandfather had been; also that in 1888, almost twenty years before her brother had been there, Gandhi had studied at the Inner Temple in London, passed the bar examination, enrolled in the High Court, then returned to India. In 1893, after two years at home, he had gone to South Africa to represent the interests of a Bombay business firm in a legal suit against the South African Government. There Gandhi had had many trying and unpleasant experiences because he was an Indian but had won the case.

During the months in South Africa, Gandhi had become increasingly concerned because his fellow countrymen had no legal rights and were often humiliated and ill treated. Shortly before he was to return to India, his friends attempted to convince him that they needed his help, as they had no strong leader. He finally agreed to stay for one more month. He remained twenty years.

It was in 1860 that Indians were first recruited as "contract labor" to work in the South African sugar fields. After five years, their contracts were fulfilled and they were sent back to India, or, if they preferred, they might remain in South Africa. Many did so and settled in or near Durban. Neither they nor their children, even if born there, were permitted to be citizens.

During these years in South Africa, Gandhi experimented with non-cooperation, the unique method through which he hoped to gain political ends by peaceful means. It was here that he evolved the term "Satyagraha." Gandhi did not like the term "passive resistance." It was too negative for him. He offered a prize for a better name. "Sadagraha" was suggested, which meant "firmness in a good cause." This Gandhi changed by combining "satya" meaning truth with "agraha," firmness or force. So it came to mean truth or love force, but since truth and love both have to do with the soul, it was more often spoken of as "soul force." It became Gandhi's goal to teach people to be strong, not through physical force but through spiritual. After twenty years in South Africa, in 1914, Gandhi returned to Bombay and very shortly identified himself with India's struggle for independence.

Nan Nehru, when she heard her father and brother discuss what Gandhi had accomplished in South Africa, little dreamed that years later she would be standing before an Assembly of the United Nations pleading the cause of the Indians of South Africa as Gandhi had pleaded their cause before she was born.

Motilal Nehru was interested in Gandhi but had little faith in his method for India. He was convinced that legal action was a far better way to bring about change. As a lawyer and a great admirer of the British and their legal system, Mr. Nehru believed implicitly that the English tradition of fair play and justice would eventually bring the government to the point where they would give his country freedom through a constitutional process. His son, however, was very critical of what was being done by the British Raj, as the government was often called, and, like most of the young intellectuals, was eager for action.

Frequently the arguments between father and son became so heated that Jawaharlal, to whom Nan was devoted, got up and left the house. He would walk for hours, arguing with himself as to what he should do. He had become increasingly interested in Gandhi's Satyagraha, although he found it extremely difficult to believe that nonviolence was more forceful and effective than striking back. It was also hard to convince himself that Gandhi was right in saying one should do good to those who opposed one, even to the extent of loving them. Nevertheless, if he had been free to do so, undoubtedly Jawaharlal would have joined Gandhi to discover more about his unusual method and whether it might be a way to secure India's independence.

These arguments disturbed Motilal Nehru, too, for he and his son were very close. For several nights, he slept on the floor in his room, since he was certain that if his son joined Gandhi, Jawaharlal would end in prison, where his bed would be hard planks. Mr. Nehru, always a practical person, decided to discover how it would feel to undergo such privations.

As the tensions in the family increased, Motilal Nehru faced what was happening and, in his direct fashion, took action. He invited Gandhi to come to Anand Bhawan for a visit. He wanted to know personally this unusual man who had such an influence on his son. Though Gandhi often seemed shy and timid, though his voice was quiet and low, Jawaharlal had discovered that there was strength in his words and that every phrase was full of meaning.

Gandhi came to Anand Bhawan. When Nan saw him, she was not impressed. Jawaharlal did not see very much of him. It was their father who had long talks with Gandhi. He even joined in the sunrise prayer meeting that Gandhi always held no matter where he was. This visit was the beginning of a long and intimate friendship between Gandhi and Motilal Nehru that all the family shared.

By the time Gandhi left, Nan had forgotten how queer he looked. At first it had been difficult for her to understand how her handsome, fastidious brother could be so attracted by this insignificant little man dressed like a peasant, wearing old steel-rimmed glasses, who ate none of the tempting dishes the cook prepared but asked for fruit, nuts, milk, and raw vegetables. Even though Nan could not understand his philosophy, she found herself more and more drawn to him. There was something intangible in Gandhi's spirit that attracted the seventeen-year-old girl. His eyes were mild but deep, and often a fierce energy and determination blazed from them. She realized that her brother was right when he said that Gandhi had "an amazing knack of reaching the hearts of people." Before leaving, Gandhi advised Jawaharlal not to give up his law work in his father's office for the present and under no circumstances to do anything to cause a break with his father. Motilal Nehru had come to admire Gandhi, but he could not accept his philosophy or political methods. Then, unexpectedly, a tragic event brought a drastic change in his thinking.

This event, however, which took place on April 6, 1919, and which welded India behind the campaign for home rule, should be understood in terms of the relations between India and England over a period of several centuries. In the history of India, there had been a long succession of invaders and conquerors. The first contact with Europe, however, was not until 1498, when the Portuguese navigator, Vasco de Gama, landed on the west coast. A few years later the Portuguese took Goa, and in 1534 the state of Bombay was ceded to them by the Sultan. It was a marriage, however, that gave the British their first claim to India. In 1662, King Charles II of England married Catherine of Braganza, a Portuguese princess. As part of her dowry, England received from Portugal the Bombay and Tangier areas of India. Later the British Commander Robert Clive defeated the Nawab of Bengal and took over the province. The chief concern of England, however, was trade. Consequently, the control of the country was left to the British East India Company, organized in 1600 to develop trade with India and the Far East. For over two hundred years India was the chief market for British goods. But these duty-free articles destroyed many of India's handicrafts, especially textile weaving. In 1857, the dissatisfaction and resentment this caused erupted in the Sepoy Mutiny. The mutiny was put down quickly, but to prevent a recurrence and to institute reforms that had long been needed, the British Government abolished the East India Company and the Crown took over control and ruled the country through a viceroy in Delhi. In 1877, as a symbol of British authority, Queen Victoria was crowned Empress of India.

A few years later, under the initiative of a retired Englishman of the Indian Civil Service, a group of Indian students who had become imbued with the British spirit of freedom, independence, and self-government while they were studying at Oxford, Cambridge, and other centers of higher learning, organized the political party known as the Indian National Congress, which had for its goal self-government. At first it was small and not very effective, but in 1920 after Gandhi became its recognized leader, it developed and became a political force throughout the country. It was to the work of this party and to Gandhi that Jawaharlal Nehru wanted to give his time and energy. The party also did much to influence Nan's future, for after she became a member, it put her to work in the field of politics, which she never left.

April 6, 1919, was declared "Satyagraha Day" by Gandhi, to be celebrated by fasting and mass meetings of protest against the Rowlatt Bills, called the "Black Bills" because they gave power to the government to act against anyone who was even suspected of working for India's independence. All business was suspended that day, and there were many demonstrations. Shortly after Satyagraha Day, two Congress party leaders were arrested in Amritsar, in the Punjab Province. Feelings ran high; people gathered to demand release of the prisoners and marched toward the European area. The police blocked their advance. There was a struggle. Several people were killed, martial law was proclaimed, and public meetings were banned.

In spite of this ban, on April 13, Hindu New Year, the Congress party held a mass meeting. Thousands gathered in Jallianwalla Bagh, a public garden, surrounded on three sides by high walls with only narrow entrances on the street side. Suddenly, during the meeting, a British general with about a hundred soldiers appeared at the main gate and ordered the crowd to leave. There was no way out. They were walled in, for the soldiers blocked the exits.

A few minutes passed, then an order rang out—"Fire!" The unarmed, panic-stricken people tried to scale the walls. Bullets struck them down. Only when the ammunition gave out, ten minutes later, did the slaughter end. Three hundred and seventy-nine Indians were killed and over a thousand wounded. Later the general responsible for the order stated that he was determined "to teach the natives a lesson."

In addition to detaining the leaders of the movement, flogging individuals under suspicion, and carrying out other oppressive measures, an order was issued that to pass through a certain lane, where an Englishwoman had been attacked, an Indian must crawl on all fours even to go to his own home. This "Crawling Order" was a turning point for Motilal Nehru. He had always admired and respected the British; he knew and practiced their laws and in many ways was a product of their traditions. But any government that would give such a humiliating order to the people of India—his people—could no longer claim his loyalty. He declared that he and his family would break with English ways. He would use all his energy to help win freedom for India. The Nehrus would follow Gandhi as their leader.

Nothing the Congress party might have done could have so effectively welded India together as did one word of a British general—"Fire!"

There were many changes at Anand Bhawan. The European area of the house was closed, there was no more luxurious entertaining, some of the household furnishings were sold, either because they were unnecessary or inappropriate for the new mode of living, and income was drastically cut. Jawaharlal gave all of his time to the Congress party, and his father took only a limited number of cases. Servants were dismissed and life was lived much more simply, although there was no lack of anything essential.

People commented that it was unbelievable a man of sixty could so radically change not only his point of view but his living habits as well. Motilal Nehru never did anything halfway. After the Amritsar tragedy, all his energy was for the cause of India's independence, and nothing else mattered.

Formerly guests arrived at Anand Bhawan in motorcars or handsome carriages. Now many came on foot. Instead of wearing elegant Indian clothes or well-tailored English suits, all who came wore garments made of *khadi*, a hand-spun, hand-woven cloth, and the men a white "Gandhi cap." Some people who previously had come to see Motilal Nehru no longer came. Those who did come were usually Congress party members. If there were women in the group, they—like Nan, Krishna, Kamala, and Mrs. Nehru—wore khadi saris and no jewelry.

To wealthy people, Gandhi said, "It's you I want, not your money." He declared he needed the help of everyone. More and more people of all castes, rich and poor, joined him. It was surprising how many of Motilal Nehru's friends also became indifferent to material comforts and took pride in living with self-denial and frugality. Nan watched her brother change. She noticed especially how he received people who came to offer help. He treated them all, no matter what their caste or economic status, with respect and dignity, even though he was sometimes impatient with them. It was remarkable to see a man, perhaps a villager, timidly enter Anand Bhawan, later to leave with assurance and confidence. Now he felt he was a part of something important for his country. As Jawaharlal expressed it, Gandhi had succeeded "in giving backbone and character" to the people of India.

An important phase of Gandhi's Satyagraha was to court arrest. Selected members of the Congress party informed the authorities that on a certain day, at a stated place and hour, they intended to shout slogans against the government and would then wait patiently until the police came to arrest them. They were given explicit instructions as to what was expected of them. "When you go," Gandhi said, "there must be no trace of anger or resentment." Also he told them, "Remember it is a privilege to go. You cannot fight for truth with hatred in your hearts, your thoughts, or your actions." The prison guards were often baffled by these prisoners and did not know how to treat them when they came in this spirit.

The changes at Anand Bhawan were difficult for the servants to understand until one of them discovered the cause. No one remembered when it had come, but for many years a cobra had lived in one of the outhouses at the rear of the compound, where wood was stored. The snake glided in and out, disturbed no one, and became an accepted part of Anand Bhawan, so much so that when a new servant was engaged, no one thought to mention the cobra to him. Shortly after his arrival, the man saw the snake and was startled and horrified. He at once killed it. He was proud of his achievement and of the good deed he felt he had done for the family he had come to serve.

Later, as the horses were sold, handsome pieces of furniture auctioned off, servants dismissed, and life drastically changed, the baffled servants kept searching for the cause of the misfortune. Then one night one of the older servants remembered the cobra. Immediately they all understood. The Nehru family must suffer retribution for the killing of the cobra. It was an act of the gods. To accept the inevitable then became easier for them.

◈ 5

◈ SWARUP KUMARI BECOMES
VIJAYA LAKSHMI

Like most Indian girls, Swarup Kumari Nehru, when she was a child, had been betrothed to a boy of about her age who belonged to a desirable, well-known family, but later this was terminated by mutual consent. As she grew into a young lady, there were various families who thought their sons suitable for the attractive daughter of the prominent lawyer. Nan, however, did not intend to have a husband selected for her, although it was customary for girls of her generation. Her liberal-minded father did not insist on arranging her marriage in spite of the fact that a few years before he had done so for his son. Consequently, when a handsome young lawyer from Kathiawar stepped into her life and asked her to share it with him, she did not hesitate to accept his offer.

The talented young man Ranjit Sitaram Pandit, then practicing law in Calcutta, was an Oxford man, about thirty years of age. He was unusually attractive, good-looking, and cultured, a great favorite wherever he went, for he made friends easily and was an asset in any group. He was familiar with both Indian and Western music, had a pleasing though untrained voice, and played the violin well. Ranjit was also a sportsman. He played cricket, polo, and tennis, swam and rode well, was a beautiful dancer, and had a reputation among his friends as a big-game hunter.

Sports were not Ranjit Pandit's chief interest, however, for although he was a lawyer, he was also a classical scholar and an historian. He enjoyed translating ancient Sanskrit plays and poems, as he was an unusual linguist. Marathi was his own language, but he also spoke Hindi, Urdu, and Persian, and soon after he opened his law office in Calcutta he was speaking Bengali fluently. Degrees from Oxford, the Sorbonne, and the University of Heidelberg had made him familiar with English, French, and German. He knew Italian also.

Ranjit Pandit had a great love of animals. He was seldom without a dog; usually he had several. Gardens were his delight—he reveled in growing things. Flowers responded to his care, and in later years, when he was a political prisoner, his garden in the jail courtyard, in spite of poor soil, always had choice flowers. All living things seemed to respond to Ranjit Pandit, especially children. Although trained for the bar at the Middle Temple in London, it was the artistic side of life that gave him the deepest satisfactions. He possessed almost every asset to make him an attractive personality and was one of the most talented among the Indian youths who studied abroad. Not many could do so, since the journey to Europe was long and costly and it was a heavy expense to a family to keep a son for four or more years in England or on the continent.

Ranjit grew up in Kathiawar in the princely state of Rajkot, where his father was a leading lawyer with a large practice and an almost unlimited income, so he was able to give his son the best education that India and Europe had to offer and an opportunity to travel over much of Europe. Consequently, when he returned to India, Ranjit Pandit had stretched his horizons to such a degree that he knew he could not settle down to married life with the average Indian girl brought up in traditional fashion, no matter how lovely she might be. He had lived abroad too long to be satisfied with an arranged marriage.

Although Ranjit Pandit went to Oxford and Jawaharlal Nehru to Cambridge, they knew each other, for Indian students frequently met in England at student gatherings. Many of the leaders of India's independence movement met that way. In their own large country, their paths might not have crossed. Like all the young men of that period who were dreaming of a free India, Ranjit looked up to Jawaharlal Nehru as his leader and wrote a tribute to him in which he expressed his deep appreciation of what he meant to the youth of India and to their country. Many of the Indian students caught their spirit of independence and their ideal of freedom from their studies in England, the country whose rule they later would struggle to overthrow.

Ranjit Pandit knew that Jawaharlal Nehru had an attractive and intelligent sister, noted for her beauty and charm, and was interested. It was probable that the daughter of the famous lawyer would be an unusual young woman, and with a brother like Jawaharlal, she undoubtedly would not be bound by tradition. He knew she had traveled more than was usual for an Indian girl. Ranjit decided to go to Allahabad to meet Swarup Kumari Nehru and decide for himself what kind of woman she might become. If Swarup was what he hoped she might be, then he would do everything he could to win her. In later years she explained his visit very simply. "I was in the marriage market," she said, "and he came my way."

To the young intellectuals of that period, Anand Bhawan had become a Mecca that all wanted to visit, especially if they were interested in law as a career or were concerned about the political struggle. Students from the university and colleges of Allahabad dropped in whenever they could. People from other parts of the province, or of India, stopped off for a few hours or a few days if they were going through Allahabad. Visitors were certain of a welcome, and the spacious house always accommodated them. Those who came not only had an opportunity to meet the Nehrus but frequently other well-known people also, who came to consult with Motilal Nehru or his son. At times there were visitors from other countries, and there was the possibility that the beloved family friend—Gandhiji—might be at Anand Bhawan. It was always a pleasure and a liberal education for the younger men to sit and listen to the discussions. Students had great admiration for Motilal Nehru, and he was an inspiration to them. Their affection, however, was for Jawaharlal, who, like them, was young, so they understood each other and they accepted him as their leader.

For old and young alike, when at Anand Bhawan, it was a delight to see the Nehru daughter, Swarup Kumari. She was always in and out, on the veranda or in the library or wherever family and guests might gather. She was not only lovely to look at but also intelligent about Congress party matters, though in her teens not too much concerned about them. One of the Allahabad University students, Triloki Nath Kaul, who often dropped in at Anand Bhawan, little dreamed that in the years to come Swarup would be an ambassador and he would work with her in Moscow and Washington and serve as her deputy high commissioner when she was India's representative in London.

Ranjit Pandit came to Anand Bhawan for other reasons than politics. He sincerely hoped that his country would one day be free and independent, but he did not feel that the political struggle was for him. He came to Allahabad unannounced but was warmly welcomed and made to feel at home. In later years Krishna in her book, *With No Regrets,* described her delight in meeting him. She was thirteen, her sister twenty. One afternoon while playing in the garden, Krishna heard someone singing. This was most unusual, for while the Nehrus were a talented family, music was not one of their assets and Motilal Nehru did not appreciate either Western or Indian music. Krishna was surprised when suddenly the door onto the veranda opened and a young man she had never seen before stepped out, saw her, and said, "Hello! I suppose you are the little sister."

She acknowledged that she was but asked, "Who are you?"

The young man replied that he was Ranjit and that he hoped they would be friends.

"But why have you come?" Krishna asked.

"To meet your sister," was Ranjit's quick response.

"What for? Why should you come all this way to meet Nan?"

Then Ranjit delighted Krishna by asking, "Can you keep a secret?"

There was nothing Krishna loved more than a secret. She straightened herself up and declared, "Certainly I can, for I'm over thirteen years old."

"Well then, I'll tell you," Ranjit said. He leaned over and whispered to her that he had come because he wanted to know and perhaps to marry Nan.

Krishna was captivated and hoped that this surprising young man would captivate Nan.

The family may have assumed that the young lawyer from Calcutta had come to Allahabad to offer his services to the Congress party. But Nan soon learned otherwise, for Ranjit Pandit knew what he wanted and why he had come. He was not entirely a stranger to Nan. Although she had never seen him before, she had read an article he had written called, "At the Feet of the Guru," which had come to her in an unexpected way.

Ranjit and Gandhi's secretary, Mahadev Desai, were good friends at Oxford. Often Mahadev would help Ranjit by criticizing what he wrote, but since their return to India, they had seen little of each other. When Ranjit heard that Mahadev was working with Gandhi, he sent him a copy of the "Modern Review" in which an article of his was published. His friend read it with much interest and shared it with Gandhi. To Mahadev's surprise, Gandhi told him that, when he was young, Ranjit's father, Sitaram Pandit, an unusual scholar, had been his *guru* or teacher, as they lived in the same city. Gandhi said he had learned much from this leading lawyer and scholar and so was interested to hear of his son. After reading the article, he casually suggested to his secretary that the next time Mahadev went to Anand Bhawan, he take the magazine with him and give it to Nan, as he thought it might interest her.

A few weeks later Desai went to Allahabad, remembered to take the magazine, and when he saw Nan, gave it to her. He told her that an article in it was written by a college friend who was a favorite in their class at Christ's College and added that Ranjit Pandit was not only a brilliant scholar but also "an unusually lovable man." Nan read the article and wondered in a vague way about the author.

Now the author was at Anand Bhawan, to meet the Nehru family and Nan. The young lawyer's stay was brief. He literally came, saw, and conquered. He arrived one day, proposed the next, and the following day was accepted. Through the happy but at times difficult years of their life together, Nan Pandit always remembered what Ranjit said to her, "I've traveled many miles and crossed many bridges to come to you. But in the future, you and I must cross our bridges hand in hand."

The wedding was to take place as soon as possible. The Nehru family was becoming increasingly involved in the independence movement and the Congress party, so was closely watched by the government. Arrests might begin shortly. It would be ironic if father and brother were in prison on Nan's wedding day.

The horoscopes of both of the young people were studied with care, and astrologers decided the tenth of May would be an auspicious day for the wedding. Preparations began at once. Relatives and friends were invited, including members of the Congress party's Working or Executive Committee. When the chairman realized the members would all be in Allahabad, to save travel expense, he called a meeting of the committee for that week. As people in the provinces heard of both the wedding and the meeting of the Working Committee, many Congress party members decided to visit Allahabad near the date, for they might catch a glimpse of party leaders whom they had never seen. Word also spread to the villages in the vicinity that the daughter of Motilal Nehru was to be married and that Gandhi would attend the wedding. Many peasants felt this was an opportune time for a pilgrimage to the sacred river, with the hope also of seeing Gandhi. Those who lived in villages where Jawaharlal Nehru had recently visited were sure the friendly young man would, on this occasion, have enough rice to share a little with them. They knew it was customary for wealthy families to feed the poor on the day of a wedding. As a result, when May 10, 1921, arrived, Allahabad was thronged with people.

Well in advance of the week of festivities, supplies were secured. Bags of rice and of spices arrived; fruits, vegetables, and legs of mutton were ordered to be delivered during the week; fresh flowers were to arrive daily. Additional servants were hired and extra ayahs to care for the women guests. Barbers and shoeshine boys were engaged. The chief problem was to be sure there were sleeping quarters to accommodate all who came. The nearest relatives were to be housed in Anand Bhawan, and a large, commodious dwelling was rented for the Pandit family with everything arranged for the comfort of Ranjit's mother. Tents were set up in the orchard; in the garden several colorful *shamianas* or marquees were erected, where guests could relax or visit. As protection from sun or rain, these spacious rectangular canopies, with one side left open, are used in India for large functions. Usually they are made of bright-colored striped canvas.

Nan's trousseau was her mother's chief concern, especially the wedding sari, which was to be as beautiful as the rarest rose, probably a heavy, embroidered brocade with a wide gold border. Saris for every possible occasion were bought—for formal and informal events, for home or for sports. It was decided that Nan should have a hundred saris in her trousseau, which meant a hundred and one, for there must always be an odd number for good luck. Everything needed to go with the sari was purchased or made—blouses, slippers, shawls (all Kashmiri ones), and jewelry that would be harmonious and appropriate for each outfit. Every morning the regular darzi, Mohammed Hussein, arrived with his assistants. As soon as the material for a sari was selected and delivered, a blouse and petticoat were made to go with it. The darzis sat cross-legged on the back veranda. Often the cloth was held between their toes, so as to leave both hands free to work the little sewing machines placed on the floor in front of them.

Hours were spent with jewelers, selecting necklaces, rings, earrings, and bangles. In India, jewelry is important both for ornamentation and as an economic asset. According to Hindu law, the jewelry given to a bride by her family or intimate friends remains hers. If for any reason a wife needs or wants money for her own use, she may sell her jewels. Consequently, every family gives to a daughter as much jewelry as they can afford.

The jewelers came to the house and spread out their many semi-precious stones for display. The precious stones they brought with them were folded in very small paper packets and kept in the owner's pocket, usually in a vest pocket. They brought to Anand Bhawan rubies and emeralds, turquoises and sapphires, amethysts and garnets, and various shades of jade. When selections were

made, clever workmen fashioned beautiful ornaments. For a few
special saris there were jeweled belts as well.

The color and texture of the wedding sari was very important.
A bride was usually married in peach, shell-pink, or red, unless the
wedding came in the spring, when the sari might be green or light
yellow. If the ceremony was to be an orthodox one, orange or dull
gold might be chosen. Mrs. Nehru had in mind an exquisite shell-
pink brocade. Then one day a letter came from Gandhi, who
wrote that he and his wife were happy about the plans and nothing would prevent their being present at the wedding. In fact,
Gandhi wrote he would be honored to give the bride away, an
idea that was quickly rejected by Motilal Nehru. What was disturbing, however, was his assumption that Swarup would be married in khadi. This was a shock. Mrs. Nehru could not think of
her beautiful daughter dressed in ugly homespun like the child of
a villager.

The wedding sari became a real problem. Motilal Nehru wanted
his daughter to be radiant and lovely, but his logical mind forced
him to see Gandhi's point. If he, Motilal Nehru, one of the outstanding leaders of the independence movement, permitted his
daughter to wear elegant cloth, either imported or domestic, the
swaraj (nationalist) movement would suffer and his part in it
seem hypocritical. Khadi, after all, had been adopted by Congress
party members to encourage local industry. If Nan's wedding
sari was made of another material, other people might also
find excuses for buying imported goods. He knew if he deserted
his principles to gratify his love for his daughter, he would seem to
be deserting the broader love of country. Gandhi, he realized, was
right when he said that independence would not be won without
personal sacrifice.

Complications set in. Each length of khadi sent to the dyers
was returned with word it would not take the dye—it was too
heavy or too coarse. No girl could be married in white, since white
was the color of mourning and was worn by widows. Mrs. Nehru
said nothing, but in her heart she must have felt that perhaps fate

was on her side after all. Her daughter might still be married in a silk sari, simpler than she had originally planned, but not coarse and ugly like khadi. At her mother's suggestion, Nan wrote Gandhi, explained the situation, and asked for his advice. There was no answer and the wedding day was near.

One morning a package arrived, addressed to Nan in Gandhi's familiar handwriting. She unwrapped it to find six yards of very fine khadi. With it came only a few lines: "For Swarup. Spun by Kasturba Gandhi with her love." Mrs. Gandhi had sent the finest of her own weaving. Off went the cloth to the dyers, this time to return a beautiful golden orange, the color of a glorious sunrise, perfect for Swarup's wedding sari.

A few days before the wedding date, relatives and friends began to arrive. For weeks gifts had poured into Anand Bhawan, both ornamental and useful. The young couple would not lack for anything. Motilal Nehru bought whatever he saw that he felt might add to Nan's comfort or happiness, including a horse and a motorcar. Her mother and aunt, aware of household needs, purchased home furnishings and kitchen utensils, many of brass, some vessels of silver. Linen from Ireland and embroidered table covers from Italy were selected. The gifts that came were a great outpouring of good will and affection, a tribute to the Nehru family and the place they held in the United Provinces and in India.

The Pandits arrived the day before the wedding, were met at the station, garlanded, and escorted to the house prepared for them. It was filled with flowers and everything imaginable for their comfort and pleasure. Ranjit's mother, older brother, two sisters, and their families came. For them it was the last wedding until the next generation began to marry, since Ranjit was the youngest of the family. Before the day was over, Ranjit sent to Swarup a beautiful box that held every article she would need for her toilet on her wedding day. On the morning of the wedding, a set of jewelry came from him, made of flowers, a symbol of the real jewels he would give her after their marriage.

Although the hot days were beginning, Wednesday, May 10, was a beautiful day with enough clouds in the sky to keep the sun's rays from beating down too intensely. For Nan the day began early. She ate no meat, only milk products and fruit, and did nothing for herself. Tradition decreed that a bride should be waited on. Seven of her unmarried friends had been selected to serve her. First she was given a ceremonial bath, when milk instead of water was poured over her body and she was rubbed with scented oils. A few days before, her hands, fingernails, and the soles of her feet had been stained with henna. This was always a gay occasion for the bride and her attendants, for fun was mixed with the ceremony. It was much more serious, on the wedding day, to tint delicately the bride's lips with betel nut and to brush her curly hair with fragrant coconut oil until it was glossy.

To drape a khadi sari was always difficult, but her friends handled Nan's with respect, for they knew Mrs. Gandhi had woven it. When it was draped, Mrs. Nehru was called, since it was always a mother's responsibility to put on her daughter's ornaments. She hung the flower garlands that Ranjit had sent around Nan's neck, fastened on the ingeniously made flower earrings, and put on the flower bangles. This done, Swarup was ready. She stood like a princess, with the women of her family and her friends grouped around her in an admiring circle. The scented oils had brought out the delicate light tint of her skin, so it was like a magnolia leaf. She was very beautiful.

A few minutes later Nan's aunt arrived carrying a tray of half-eaten food. It came from Ranjit. Part of the wedding tradition was for the groom to share his first meal of the day with his bride-to-be.

Some little time before the ceremony, the Pandit family arrived. Had it been in earlier days, there would have been a procession, with the groom mounted on a white horse, a band, and an elephant whose trunk and ears would have been decorated with a painted design for the occasion. Now the Pandits came in motor-cars. They were received by Mrs. Nehru and other relatives, who welcomed them with trays heaped with flowers or with lighted lamps and incense. Swarup appeared only long enough to garland Ranjit, then quickly left. The Pandit party was escorted into the house; refreshments were brought, the men being served in one room, the women in another. All were entertained with music and talk until the auspicious hour for the wedding ceremony arrived.

While these preparations were going on in the house, there was a commotion at the gate. The *chowkidar* or watchman sent word for Jawaharlal Nehru to come at once. He hurried out to find the police there. He thanked them for coming but informed them that their services were not needed, as the Anand Bhawan chowkidars would be able to handle the crowd. He told them that the several hundred people there were all relatives, friends, or members of the Congress party's Working Committee.

"That's just it," a surly policeman replied. "What do you mean having all your Congress party leaders here for a wedding? If you are planning a demonstration, we want you to know we'll put down any disturbance without a moment's notice. We are here to warn you and protect the city."

Jawaharlal Nehru was amazed and asked why there should be a demonstration.

"Don't pretend you are so ignorant. You know what day this is."

He was even more puzzled. Then suddenly he remembered. It was on May 10, 1857, that the Sepoy Mutiny had broken out against the British. Ever since, the police had been watchful on that day. They were doubly so now, for they knew the Congress party leaders were at Anand Bhawan and several hundred peasants were camped near the river. Orders were sent to all Britishers in Allahabad that it might be well to carry their rifles if they went out during the day. Secret service men were watching what went

on at Anand Bhawan. The police authorities believed that the political trouble makers might plan something under the guise of a
wedding.

Jawaharlal Nehru explained to the Chief of Police that the day's
festivities had nothing to do with the mutiny, only with the horoscopes of the bride and groom. He gave his word that there would
be no disturbance and asked the police to leave, as it was almost
time for the ceremony.

"I hope you are telling the truth," the chief replied. "We'll
leave, but I warn you we will be watching until the last guest has
gone."

From early morning, musicians, recruited from all over the
province, played in various parts of the large compound. There
were trumpets and clarinets, drums and cymbals, and the
shahanai, an instrument similar to a bagpipe, which added a
somber note to the gay, jubilant music. As the time for the ceremony drew near, guests came forward in the garden and crowded
onto the verandas.

A simplified version of the ancient orthodox Kashmiri wedding
ceremony was used. On thick rugs, the priests seated themselves
cross-legged in a circle. In the center was a sacred wood fire to be
lighted on the ground. In India, to be binding, vows are made
over a fire. If so made, no marriage certificate is necessary, for any
court respects these vows. A young priest placed the various
utensils conveniently near the eldest priest. A silver spoon, the
puja vessels, the bowls with the sacred water brought that morning from the Ganges, and the incense burners were all properly
arranged.

A hush fell on the guests as Motilal Nehru and his wife came
out of the house with Swarup. There were exclamations of surprise as the daughter of the wealthy lawyer appeared dressed in
khadi and comments of approval from the Congress party members. Many surmised this was Gandhi's influence. They knew that,
if possible, he would turn any occasion into an event for the na-

tional cause, even a wedding. There were universal exclamations of delight as the guests saw how beautiful Swarup Kumari was on her wedding day.

Eyes cast down, Swarup seated herself on the deep cushion close to the cushion on which her father sat. Her mother was on the other side of him, the mother's presence being evidence of her consent to the marriage and her part in the giving away of their daughter. From the opposite direction came Ranjit Pandit. Many were eager to see this stranger, who, although Brahman, was neither Kashmiri nor of the United Provinces, yet had won the Nehru daughter. Erect, handsome, serious, yet with a twinkle in his eye and a slight smile as he caught sight of Swarup, the son of the Rajput family of Pandit, also dressed in khadi, walked to the circle and gracefully seated himself on the carpet beside the priest, his bride to be on the opposite side of the fire.

When the participants were seated and the guests quiet, the eldest priest lighted the sacred fire, since Vedic times the emblem of purity. Slowly he fed it chips of scented wood and incense. Then he dipped the silver spoon into melted butter and let it drip onto the fire. He added perfumed salts until the fire crackled and sizzled. In a few minutes the air was filled with a strong aromatic scent as the fragrance of the incense drifted through the garden. As he tended the fire, the priest and other pundits, in soft, plaintive, almost melancholy voices, chanted ancient Vedic hymns.

When the fire was burning brightly, the priest asked who was to give the bride away. Motilal Nehru answered and, in the time-honored "giving-away ceremony," took the hand of his daughter and placed it in the hand of Ranjit, stretched out to receive it. With their hands crossed over the fire, they repeated their vows after the priest. Then they rose and seven times walked around the fire as the priest chanted, repeating their promises to live according to Hindu tradition; to be true to each other and share each other's burdens; to live together for the welfare of the family, community, and country; to beget sons and so propagate the race;

and, last of all, to remain forever faithful to each other and firm
as a rock. The Seven Rounds finished, the couple sat side by side
while the priest chanted a final admonition:

> "As Rama was to Sita
> So may the husband be to his bride."

One verse Nan always remembered:

> "May you have wealth and many sons,
> May you always be beloved by your husband.
> In wisdom and humility may you both
> Serve the community for a hundred years."

Lastly, Ranjit and Swarup, now husband and wife, sat facing
each other with a scarf thrown over their heads. Parents and
friends surrounded them and showered them with rose petals
while the final blessing was chanted.

The ceremony over, the musicians again filled the compound
with music, the feast was served, and Anand Bhawan overflowed
with gay chatter, delicious food, and much good will.

Ranjit at once took his bride to his mother and the Pandit relatives to be accepted into their family. Nan gave each one of the
men of the family a sweet, and they in return gave her their blessing. Then one of the priests gave to her the new name that the
Pandit family had chosen for her. It must correspond to the husband's name. Since Ranjit means "Victor," it seemed appropriate
to call Swarup the "Conquering Goddess"—Vijaya Lakshmi. It
is not necessary for the bride to use the new name unless she
wishes to do so. Her husband's family will always use it, but her
own family and friends need not. Swarup Kumari liked this new
name and gladly accepted it, though she admitted it was quite a
change to become Vijaya Lakshmi Pandit instead of Nan Nehru.
In later years, when young admirers asked for her autograph, she
often commented upon the amount of time her lengthy signature
required.

Later in the day, Vijaya Lakshmi and her attendants slipped

away so that she could change her sari for the wedding picture. She put on a sari of heavy gold tissue, embroidered with jewels. The girls arranged strings of pearls across the back of her head, up and down the part in her hair, and across her forehead, braided her hair with a gold cord, fastened it with jeweled pins, and put on her choicest earrings, necklaces, and bangles. Her mother, father, and Ranjit also changed into elaborate costumes. Then they went into the drawing room, where the photographer was waiting to take a picture of the handsome couple and their parents.

After the wedding festivities, the bride and groom left for Calcutta, their wedding trip postponed until later in the year when they planned to go to Europe. Before they left Anand Bhawan, they went to Gandhi's room to have a brief visit and to receive his blessing.

As they were to be in Calcutta only three months, they took temporary quarters and lived a carefree life with many social functions. It was the hot season. There were garden parties, picnics, and events at the boating clubs. Life was gay and happy for the popular young couple, and Vijaya Lakshmi, as people now called her, soon made a place for herself in the new setting. In September, they set sail for the belated honeymoon, which was spent in London, Paris, Heidelberg, and other of Ranjit's favorite European cities.

◆ 6

◆ THE PANDITS ENTER THE
CONGRESS PARTY

Back again in Calcutta, early in 1922, Vijaya Lakshmi and Ranjit found a house and settled down to creating a home of their own. The days went happily for them except when there was disquieting news from Allahabad. They had been in Europe when Nan's father and, shortly afterwards, her brother were arrested for their independence activities. Now it was disturbing to learn that Jawaharlal, after being released, had been arrested a second time. At Christmastime, while Nan was abroad, her mother had gone to the annual Congress party meeting in Ahmedabad and had traveled third class, an almost unbelievable thing for Mrs. Nehru to do. Mrs. Nehru, Kamala, with five-year-old Indira, and Krishna had all gone together. To picture her dainty, delicate mother in a cramped and crowded third-class compartment was almost impossible for Nan, but it was another example of the changes Gandhi had made in the life of the Nehrus.

In March, 1924, while in Bombay for a short time, a dream came true for the Pandits. Nan felt their first-born child must be a son; Ranjit hoped for a girl and had a name selected for her— Chandralekha or "The Crescent." When a daughter arrived, Ranjit was overjoyed. A tiny crescent moon appeared in the sky that night. At home in Calcutta, the days were busy and full of joy as together they watched their small daughter grow, heard her say her first words, and take her first steps.

Three years later, Nan Pandit was occupied with a new concern. Lekha, she hoped, was to have a brother. Ranjit again wanted a girl. He felt a sister would be much nicer for Lekha. He had been lonely as a child because his brother was much older, and he had always wished for a playmate. Nan Pandit went home to Anand Bhawan to wait for the new arrival. It gave her a feeling of contentment to realize that twenty-seven years before she had been born in the same room where her child would be born. To make the occasion more eventful, the baby arrived on May 10, her wedding day. To Ranjit's delight it was another daughter, whom he named Nayantara, which meant "Star of the Eye."

The next year, Ranjit decided that Nan needed a change and he needed a holiday. They left the children in Allahabad with Nan's mother and Krishna and went to Europe. It was a delightful trip, but this time there were two tiny but strong threads pulling them back to India.

Home again and the children collected from Allahabad, life went on much as usual in Calcutta. Ranjit was busy at his law office, Nan with the home and the children. They had returned to India in time for the 1928 annual convention of the Congress party at which Nan's father, Motilal Nehru, would preside. Since it was in Calcutta, Mrs. Nehru, Kamala, and Krishna all planned to come, and Jawaharlal Nehru would be in the thick of it. Ranjit secured a house nearby to accommodate the family.

The Congress session was not an easy one for them because father and son did not agree on the tactics for the future action of the party. Jawaharlal Nehru wanted a strong, dynamic independence motion, while his father wished to proceed with caution. Finally, a compromise was worked out. The report that the elder Nehru approved included items from his son's resolution. The convention decided that if, within a year, the British Government did not agree to what was called the "All Parties Constitution" for a completely free and independent India, the Congress party would take strong action at the next convention.

Nan Pandit watched with interest the way in which her father presided over the difficult session and was pleased when her brother was again elected General Secretary of the party. But what amazed all the family was the strength their mother seemed to have acquired. She sat for long hours, often through dull discussions and speeches in English, which she did not understand. She was delighted when the audience broke into applause or cheered some point her husband made, even though she often had no idea why they did so.

Life in Calcutta was a happy one for the Pandits. Still Nan was not entirely satisfied. She often longed to be back in the United Provinces, in her home in Allahabad, where she felt she was at the heart of the Congress party movement. She knew vital, important things were taking place in India, yet she and Ranjit were removed from them. Nan Pandit wanted to be closer to what was going on and to what concerned her father, her brother, and Kamala. In the United Provinces she felt more conscious of the new India about to come into being.

At first it seemed almost impossible to Ranjit Pandit that he consider giving up his law practice and enter the political world. He felt he had neither the training nor the inclination. He was not a crusader like the Nehrus, and while he belonged to the Congress party, he was not one of Gandhi's ardent followers, although he deeply admired and respected him. Nevertheless, like his wife, he wanted their children to grow up in a free India. The days were difficult, with much discussion of what was the wise thing to do. At one point Ranjit made the suggestion that they simplify their living and so be able to make a larger contribution to the Congress party treasury. He felt he might be more useful in this way. Gandhi's words, however, kept coming back to them—that what he wanted was the people themselves, not their money.

Ranjit Pandit was a scholar who would rather translate a book than make a speech and who knew he would prefer to spend his days in the British Museum rather than in a British jail. Yet Nan's happiness meant more to him than anything else. No matter what his sacrifice, it would be nothing to what he would feel if he were blocking her in what she wanted to do. In the end, it was decided that they would give up the Calcutta home, Ranjit would leave his law office, and they would live in Allahabad. Nan hoped they might live in her beloved Anand Bhawan, so full of memories, where they both could be more closely identified with the independence movement. Years later, she admitted that her husband had been almost "dragged into" work for the party. Yet it had come to be a choice for him between "bondage or freedom of spirit." In this, Ranjit Pandit knew there was only one decision to make. They left Calcutta and established their home in Allahabad.

A disappointment, however, was in store for Nan Pandit. Her father had decided to give his home, Anand Bhawan, to the Congress party for its national headquarters. He felt it was not in keeping with Gandhi's ideas for him to live in such luxury. Gandhi talked of sacrifice while the Nehrus were living not in one but in two large houses. So Motilal Nehru, although he had not made it public as yet, decided that he, his wife, and Krishna would move into the home he had built for Jawaharlal and Kamala. The older house would become the property of the party, which had never had satisfactory offices. He hoped this would help the political movement and give more dignity to the party. Motilal Nehru could not give up the name, Anand Bhawan, however. It was to be transferred to Jawaharlal's house while the former home would be renamed "Swaraj Bhawan," or "Freedom House." Here Pundit Nehru hoped the new India would come into being. The house where his daughters and granddaughter had been born would become the birthplace of his country. As the Americans had their Mount Vernon, the home of Washington, so the Nehru home might some day be the "Mount Vernon of India."

This change meant that the Pandits had to begin their life in Allahabad in a new setting. A satisfactory house was found a short distance from Anand Bhawan. Here Ranjit Pandit passed on to his daughters the Kathiawar traditions of his family and Nan the Kashmiri customs of the Nehrus. The children grew up enriched by the heritage of both.

It was the end of October, 1929, when Lekha was five years old and Tara two, that Nan Pandit told her father, "Of course it will be a girl. I've given up hoping for a son." And it was. Ranjit was again delighted and had a name for their third daughter. To the other girls he had given poetic names. Now life for the Pandits had taken a more realistic turn, for they were closely involved in their country's struggle. Gandhi kept reminding the people of India that, in the days ahead, they must hold fast to truth, so her father called the baby Rita, meaning "Truth."

When it was time for the 1929 Congress party meeting, which was to be held in Lahore, the leaders anticipated that it might be an explosive occasion, since the constitution drawn up by the political parties of India had not been accepted by the British Government. Also, it was the tenth anniversary of the Jallianwalla Bagh massacre in nearby Amritsar. Consequently, the choice of the new president was of unusual importance. The Nehrus and most of the party members assumed the central committee would nominate Gandhi.

During the past year, Gandhi had done little for the party. Instead he had traveled all over India by train and car, by cart and on foot. Every few miles crowds gathered, if only to be able to return to their homes and say, "I saw him! I saw Mahatma Gandhi! With my own eyes I have seen our Gandhiji!" This was enough. From others they could learn what he said, but to look for even a fleeting moment at the man they reverenced was important. Gandhi did not talk of independence; he urged them to spin and to wear khadi. Many Congress party leaders believed it was wasted effort, but Gandhi knew that even the poorest villagers could spin, and if at the same time they felt that by doing this they were helping to make a better life for their children, it would add strength to the struggle.

Although all the provincial committees nominated Gandhi for the presidency, he refused and recommended that a man be chosen from the younger members of the party. "Youth must play its part," he said, and urged that someone about forty years of age be selected. To the surprise and delight of the Nehrus, he informed the party that his choice was Jawaharlal Nehru. To those who considered Jawaharlal too inexperienced, Gandhi said, "If he has the dash and rashness of a warrior, he also has the prudence of a statesman. . . . The nation is safe in his hands."

With pride, Motilal Nehru, as retiring president, passed on the gavel to his son. The Nehru family was in Lahore to see him do so in his most regal manner. Nan was devoted to her brother, and it was a delight to her when she heard people say that this was only a beginning. Jawaharlal Nehru would some day be one of the great leaders of India. Her only disappointment was that two-month-old Rita kept her from taking part in the celebration.

The three hundred thousand Congress party delegates lived in an enormous tent camp on the banks of the Ravi River, a short distance from Lahore. Here the Youth League claimed Jawaharlal Nehru as its special leader and made the opening day a gala occasion. The group secured a white horse for him to ride and a score of elephants for the procession.

On the last day of 1929, thunderous shouts and applause broke out when exactly at midnight the resolution demanding complete independence was passed unanimously. The annual conference closed with thousands of members gathered by the river. Led by their new president, Jawaharlal Nehru, they recited the Pledge of Swaraj, the independence pledge, and dedicated themselves to their country's cause.

The time for action had now come. January 26, 1930, had been chosen as Independence Day. Mass meetings were to be held throughout India during the year. All were to close with the reading of the Pledge of Swaraj, which began with a declaration that freedom was the inalienable right of the Indian people, as of any people, and that they recognized the most effective way to gain freedom was through nonviolence. A solemn pledge for civil disobedience followed. In Allahabad, Nan and Ranjit were among those who pledged themselves to more active participation in the movement.

Gandhi had proclaimed Satyagraha but had given no instructions. He never acted until the next step was clear to him. Those who knew him best began to wonder if the inner voice on which he depended for inspiration had failed to speak. A month went by. The country waited. Then Gandhi's pronouncement came. It was salt! Congress party members and people in general were to disobey the government by making salt. The making of salt was a government monopoly, and there was a purchase tax on it. Since salt was a necessity, Gandhi had asked that the tax be abolished, but the British Viceroy took no notice of his request. Many thought that Gandhi's idea was fantastic and asked how independence could be won by defying the government in regard to salt. Others felt it was a clever move that would catch the imagination of the masses because everyone must have salt. It might help to unite the people of India if they struggled together for a simple, basic need. The Congress party published an instruction pamphlet. A frequent request among friends was, "Please lend me your salt pamphlet." Salt became a magic word, as people all over India prepared to make it.

One day the Pandit children found their grandfather surrounded by pots and pans. "Grandpa, what are you doing?" Lekha asked.

Motilal Nehru straightened up and proudly announced, "I am learning to make salt."

With his instinct for the dramatic, Gandhi decided that for the first salt-making demonstration, he would walk the two hundred and forty-one miles to the Arabian Sea from his *ashram* near Ahmedabad in western India. (An ashram is a colony or spiritual retreat where a leader lives with his disciples.) So on March 12, 1930, after a sunrise prayer meeting, seventy-eight of his followers started. Staff in hand, Gandhi led them. In each town and village through which they went, crowds greeted them, and many walked on with Gandhi to the next village.

On April 5, Gandhi reached the Arabian Sea, his party now augmented by those who were eager to be present when the salt law was broken. Gandhi paused for his early morning prayer meeting, then led his chosen followers to the water's edge and symbolically claimed the salt from the sea as India's birthright. Everyone expected that Gandhi would immediately be arrested, but this did not happen.

All over the country, shops where British goods were sold were picketed and boycotted. Gandhi called upon the women especially to picket. Kamala and Krishna responded immediately; Nan joined them whenever she could leave the children. For the present, they were her first responsibility. To the distress of Mrs. Nehru, her daughters wore trousers for picketing instead of saris. They found it easier to move about in them and, if necessary, to lie down across a shop doorway to prevent people from entering to buy British goods. Many of the stores voluntarily closed; others were forced to do so.

Picketing was a new and strange experience for the Nehru sisters. They had seldom gone to the bazaars, the market places, in the poorer sections of Allahabad and were amazed to discover that sections of their city were so ugly and dirty, with people living in the midst of filth and poverty. It was astonishing to Nan Pandit to realize that, though she was thirty years of age, this was the first time she had really seen the city in which she had lived most of those years. Gandhi was right. What she and others like her needed to do was to wake up to what was happening to the people of their country.

A few days after the Salt March, the police came to Anand Bhawan to arrest the president of the Indian National Congress. Hastily, Jawaharlal Nehru issued a statement that during his enforced absence, his father, Motilal Nehru, would serve as acting president of the Congress. Jawaharlal was sentenced to six months in prison.

A month passed. Then, when no one was expecting it, at one o'clock in the morning, the police came and rushed Gandhi to Yeravda Prison near Poona. For a short time, only a few at his ashram knew he was gone. In the morning news of the arrest spread, and people reacted vigorously. In Bombay, fifty thousand mill workers walked off their jobs; merchants proclaimed a *hartal*, when shops were closed as a form of passive resistance. No one purchased British goods; business was paralyzed.

The government retaliated with mass arrests. In a short time, sixty thousand Indians were in prison, women as well as men, boys and girls also. The jails were jammed; prison staffs were desperate. It was a new experience to handle prisoners who came garlanded and singing, apparently happy to be arrested.

One afternoon at teatime, the Pandit children were chatting gaily with their father when there was a commotion at the door and a policeman entered and announced that Ranjit was under arrest. He left the room to get the few things he was permitted to take with him. For Lekha, now six years old, this was a new experience. "Mummie, what does that man want?" she asked in a loud whisper. Her mother replied that it was nothing important; he had only come to take their father to prison. A few minutes later, with bag in hand and an armful of books, Ranjit Pandit departed.

"Now, children," Nan Pandit said, "we have chocolate cake to celebrate; Papu has gone to prison." Years later, Tara used this incident for the title of her first book, *Prison and Chocolate Cake*. The two had been closely linked in her three-year-old mind.

Although he was troubled by asthma and sometimes his heart acted queerly, Nan Pandit's father kept doggedly at work at the party office in Swaraj Bhawan, his old home. On the night of June 30, 1930, after all were asleep at the new Anand Bhawan, the police came for Mr. Nehru. "Aren't you a little late in arriving?" he asked them. "I've been expecting your call for weeks." Laughing and joking, Motilal Nehru said good-by to his wife and departed.

Ten weeks went by, and each visitor's day Nan and her mother, with Kamala and Krishna, went to Naini Jail. Fortunately, Motilal Nehru was put with Jawaharlal and Ranjit, but they were concerned about him, as he was far from well. When there were suggestions that his release be requested because of his health, Motilal Nehru reacted vehemently and declared that no special privileges should be asked for him. Eventually, the officials became disturbed also, and to Nan's relief, in early September, Motilal Nehru was unconditionally discharged. Nan immediately took her mother, father, and the children to the hill station of Mussoorie, where, in the clear cool mountain air, her father's health began to improve.

A month later, there was again good news. Jawaharlal Nehru was released, and after several busy days in Allahabad, he and Kamala joined the family in Mussoorie. Here father and son had time for leisurely talk, short walks, and much enjoyment of the children. Motilal Nehru chuckled and clapped his hands with delight as Jawaharlal, like a small boy, marched around the living room with his daughter and Nan's three small girls. Lekha carried the Congress party flag and led the procession as they tramped and sang party songs.

After three days, Jawaharlal and Kamala returned to Allahabad, and a day later, fearful his son might be rearrested, Motilal Nehru also returned. Jawaharlal met him at the station, then hurried off to a meeting, promising he would see his father that evening. The meeting over, weary from the strain of the busy day, Jawaharlal and Kamala started home. A short distance from the gate of Anand Bhawan, their car was stopped, Jawaharlal was ordered out and into a waiting car, and, with no explanation, was driven to Naini Jail.

Kamala was stunned by the suddenness of what had happened but went on to Anand Bhawan, where she had the difficult task of telling her father-in-law what had occurred. The news was a terrible shock to him, for Motilal Nehru had been counting on the evening with his son. "No! No! Not so soon!" he kept saying. Then to everyone's amazement, he straightened himself in his chair, banged the table in front of him, and declared that he would not be ill, that he would go on with the work that must be done. He stood up with more vigor than he had shown for months, and the following morning he was at work early. For several days he seemed to have his former energy and went to the prison for a talk with his son. He issued several statements and conferred with many people, which gave new vitality to the civil disobedience workers. "Isn't it wonderful," people said, "to have Motilal Nehru at the helm again." For November 14, his son's birthday, he organized "Jawahar Day," when at public meetings all over India people read portions of the speech that had been responsible for Jawaharlal's arrest. For Jawaharlal Nehru it was an unusual birthday celebration.

There was, unfortunately, no reserve of strength behind the will of Motilal Nehru. His body had done all it could; he was ill and utterly exhausted. He was persuaded to go with Krishna to Calcutta to take a short sea trip. When they reached there, the doctors advised against it, so he settled down in Calcutta for a time. Then came word that Kamala was arrested. "They mustn't put Kamala in jail!" Motilal Nehru exclaimed. "They mustn't!" He knew she had overtaxed her strength in order to carry on after Jawaharlal's arrest. In a few days Krishna and her father returned to Allahabad, and in the meantime Nan and the children had come down from Mussoorie.

January of 1931 was a special month for the Nehru household. Kamala had been released and, soon after, Jawaharlal and Ranjit were also. When he arrived home, Jawaharlal went directly to his father's room. He was shocked by his appearance and could think of nothing to say to his father as he embraced him. Immediately he sent a telegram to Gandhi, who left everything to come at once to Allahabad. Motilal Nehru's face fairly glowed when he saw Gandhiji standing beside him. Having him there gave Nan and the family a feeling of hope and peace. Yet it was an effort for Pundit Nehru to joke with his friend as he always had done in the past.

News of the illness of Motilal Nehru spread. Many friends came to Anand Bhawan as soon as they were released from prison, even before going to their own homes. The famous lawyer, formerly a man of vigor on whom many had leaned for support, only had strength to give them a fleeting smile. As he grew weaker, the doctors decided he should be taken to Lucknow for special treatment. He begged to remain at home, for he wanted his last days to be at Anand Bhawan. The doctors appealed to Gandhi to decide what should be done. It was a difficult decision. He understood Motilal Nehru's feelings, yet he believed if there was the slightest possibility of keeping his friend even a little longer, they should take the chance. So Gandhi agreed with the doctors. Pundit Nehru was too weak to protest any more.

The family went with him, the long drive a trying ordeal for all. The following day, when their father seemed better, it was agreed that Gandhi had been right—the change might lengthen his life. But Motilal Nehru's final journey was drawing to an end. On the evening of February 6, 1931, it was over. His wife gave one cry of unutterable grief, then sat huddled in a corner of the room, completely crushed. Nan and Krishna were overcome with grief, while Jawaharlal stood speechless.

A few minutes later Gandhi entered the room, sat beside Mrs. Nehru, and put his hand lovingly on her shoulder. Quietly, with great tenderness, he said, "Your husband is not dead. He will live long." Gandhi's simple words brought tears of release and comfort to the stricken family.

In the next hours, word of the death of Motilal Nehru spread. In the morning, hundreds of people flocked to Kalakanker Palace, where the family was staying. Nan and Krishna went on ahead to Allahabad. Jawaharlal and Ranjit brought the body draped in a national flag. Gandhi and Mrs. Nehru followed a little later. All the way to Allahabad, the road was lined with people. Many waited hours to pay their last respects to one of their most esteemed leaders. In Allahabad, the cars could hardly move because of the throng. As the car with the body of Motilal Nehru crept through the gates of Anand Bhawan, there welled up from the crowd a great heartbreaking murmur.

When everything was ready, devoted friends carried the flower-covered bier to the Ganges River. On the way the procession grew and grew until a hundred thousand people were surging down the road. As tradition decreed, Jawaharlal, the son, rendered his last service for his father when he lighted the funeral pyre. The scent of sandalwood filled the air as the great crowd stood silent.

The last rites over, Gandhi spoke to the throng of people and urged them not to rest until the freedom of India was achieved.

He ended, "This was the cause dearest to the heart of Motilalji. It was for this he gave his life."

At Anand Bhawan the women sat and waited, each with her memories of the great man whose life was now ended, though they knew that what Gandhi had said would be true—he would live on in all of them. Nan Pandit, so like her father, little realized the degree to which he would live on in her as she took her place in the political life of India.

◆ 7

◆ THE NEHRU SISTERS GO
  TO PRISON

For weeks messages of condolence, hundreds of them, came from all over India and from many countries of the world, but the days of mourning for Motilal Nehru were few. The family knew he would want it so. Ranjit Pandit had to leave Nan and the children and return to prison. Fortunately, Jawaharlal Nehru, now the head of the family, could remain at home, since the members of the Congress's Working Committee, made up of the officers of the Congress party and about a dozen other provincial representatives, had been unconditionally released. The committee set to work in their new national headquarters, Swaraj Bhawan. Pundit Nehru's unprecedented gift not only made their work easier but also kept his spirit alive among them.

The delegates returning from a round-table conference held in London to discuss the future relationship between Britain and India had landed in Bombay on the very day that Motilal Nehru died. They hurried to Allahabad to present their report to the working committee. After a lengthy discussion, it was decided that Gandhi should ask to see the Viceroy, Lord Irwin. The request was granted, and Gandhi left for Delhi, where the committee joined him later. Many of the members were not very happy about the agreement Gandhi and Lord Irwin worked out. They felt Gandhi had accepted a statement that was too vague. It did not say clearly that India's goal was *purna swaraj*—complete independence—and it gave India little in return for the promise Gandhi made to call off civil disobedience.

The conference over, Jawaharlal and Ranjit, now released, were occupied almost immediately in sending out from Swaraj Bhawan instructions to stop civil disobedience. All over India, according to agreement, Congress party members were discharged from prisons. Frequently they irritated the authorities, for they would be driven through the streets, garlanded and singing. "They act as though they had won a victory!" one of the police said. The Congress party members believed they had, because the struggle had raised the people of India in their own estimation. Even the youngest volunteers, the children, held their heads high with pride. Newsmen reported that at last India had caught the attention of the international press and that this world interest would help India's cause.

There was a large attendance at the 1931 annual session of the Congress party, held in March in Karachi. It was a long trip. To reach there, the Nehrus went from Allahabad to Lahore, then across the hot, dusty Sind Desert. To their amazement, Mrs. Nehru went with them. In spite of the distance, there was a large attendance. At this session the Congress adopted a resolution that meant much to Gandhi, for it dealt with the abolition of untouchability. Gandhi insisted that India must no longer use the terms "untouchables," "outcastes," or "depressed classes," as the people at the bottom of India's age-old caste system had been called. Instead, these people were to be called "Harijans," which meant "Children of God."

Home again in Allahabad, Ranjit and Nan decided that their oldest daughter Lekha, now seven, should go to school. After considering various possibilities, they selected a friend's private school near Poona, south of Bombay, where her father would take her. Although it was almost more than she could stand to say good-by to her mother, Lekha felt proud and important going off alone with her father. In the compartment before the train started, she sat up very straight, her small feet not touching the floor, unrolled a package, pulled out a long stick, and proudly held up a Congress flag.

"What are you doing with that?" her mother asked.

"It's to keep the police away!" Lekha calmly replied, clutching the flag more firmly.

As the train started, Ranjit called to Nan, "Don't worry about us. Lekha and her flag will keep us safe."

A few months later, as the political situation became more complicated and uncertain, the Pandits faced the fact that in the days ahead not only Ranjit but possibly Nan as well might be arrested, for now that the baby was older, she had increased her Congress party work. If this happened, the question was who would look after the two children at home. Rita was not quite two, Tara only four. It was a most difficult decision to make, but the parents finally decided it was wise to take the children to join their older sister in Poona, leaving them at the school in the care of their friend. It was heartbreaking to part with them, but it helped when, in Poona, Lekha told her mother good-by and said, "Don't worry, Mummie; we'll be all right. I'll look after Tara and the baby."

Back in Allahabad, the house was quiet and empty. There were no shrill young voices to greet their parents, no happy faces waiting for them, no one to be concerned whether or not there was cake for tea. With more leisure, Nan Pandit threw herself into whatever work the Congress party asked her to do. It was, however, mainly a period of waiting until the second round-table conference was over in London.

Finally, the first of December, 1931, the meetings were adjourned with little accomplished. Gandhi returned to India, eager to meet the Congress leaders, especially Jawaharlal Nehru.

When the boat docked in Bombay, Gandhi looked down on the crowd below to find Nehru, for he was sure he would be there. He could not locate him and wondered what had happened.

When on shore, the news came. Two days before, Jawaharlal had left Allahabad on the express train to be in Bombay when Gandhi arrived. After a short run, the train halted at a small station, not a regular stop. The police came directly to Nehru's compartment and hustled him and his traveling companion, Sherwani, into a waiting automobile. Immediately, without trial, both men were sentenced. Although their offenses were the same, Sherwani was given six months' imprisonment, Nehru two years', with a fine of five hundred rupees and the stipulation that if the fine was not paid, six months would be added to the prison sentence.

Gandhi's disappointment when the information reached him was intense. It was even more so after he heard of the recent exceptionally stringent regulations that even the British Secretary of State for India, Sir Samuel Hoare, admitted to the House of Commons were drastic and severe. Gandhi knew the situation was deteriorating rapidly and was concerned as to what could be done about it. There was no time for him to plan anything. A week later Gandhi himself was arrested and held without trial. Then the government struck hard. The Congress party was outlawed, its records destroyed, its funds confiscated, its buildings seized. At Anand Bhawan, Nan Pandit and Krishna wondered what would happen next. They soon knew. A government order was delivered that informed Vijaya Lakshmi Pandit and Krishna Nehru that, under penalty of arrest, they were not to participate in any public demonstration for one month. The communication was not entirely unexpected, for they were working on plans for the Allahabad Independence Day celebration to be held in less than a month's time.

Mrs. Pandit accepted the notification from the police officer without comment. He asked if she understood what it meant. She replied that she did. As a result of this, the committee was even more determined that the celebration must be an impressive one Allahabad would never forget. As a precaution, for the two weeks preceding the date, the Nehru sisters did no work out in the city.

A few days later, at Anand Bhawan, Nan, Krishna, and the other members of the committee were discussing who should preside at the mass meeting. Several names were suggested, but for various reasons the people did not qualify or were in prison. Then unexpectedly, Mrs. Nehru, who had been listening to the discussion, said she would be glad to preside. Her daughters were amazed, for this was something their mother had never done before.

The news spread. "Have you heard?" people said. "Motilal Nehru's widow is to preside at the Independence Day meeting." It was almost impossible to believe that this delicate woman, who all her life had been sheltered and protected, was to chair a great mass meeting. The Congress party members were all determined to be there to give her support.

January 26, 1932, arrived. Everywhere in India, Congress members gathered in overflow meetings. In Allahabad no one could remember such a crowd of people for a political gathering. Mrs. Nehru not only presided but, to the astonishment of her family and friends, made an impassioned speech that brought forth tremendous applause. A tiny figure, she stood on a platform especially made to raise her high enough for people to see her and spoke from her heart.

During the day there were a few *lathi* charges to control the crowd. Lathis were long bamboo sticks carried by the police. To the surprise of everyone concerned, nothing else happened. The celebration over, the Nehrus returned home to Anand Bhawan, amazed that neither Nan nor Krishna had been arrested.

The next morning Mrs. Nehru slept late. About nine-thirty a knock on her door aroused her. The bearer had come to tell her that the police had arrived and were asking for her daughters. In her room Nan Pandit was stirring around leisurely when the bearer came to tell her that the police were waiting below for her and her sister. Mrs. Pandit dressed quickly, went downstairs and out onto the veranda, where a police officer was waiting. He handed her an official envelope. She tore it open. She and Krishna were under arrest. An information sheet with the order stated that six saris and a few underclothes was the extent of clothing allowed. These were soon packed; farewells were said and servants given last instructions.

"We are ready," Mrs. Pandit said as she and Krishna went down the steps and into the police van. As they drove out of the gates, they looked back. Their mother stood on the veranda, her hands still held in the Indian gesture of farewell.

Nan and Krishna knew the prison well, for they had come many times to visit members of their family and friends, but this was the first time the gates had swung open for them to enter not as visitors but as inmates. Formalities began at once. They were weighed; their bags were inspected and instructions given. There were no regular women's quarters. Instead, as soon as women were sentenced, they were sent to other prisons. Consequently, in the yard reserved for women, political prisoners were jumbled together with seasoned criminals and others there for lesser crimes. As the Nehru sisters entered the yard, they were eagerly greeted by the political prisoners who had arrived earlier that day. They met like long-lost friends rather than Congress members who only the day before had been working together. Nan and Krishna had to share a small cell with two other women. It was filthy; vermin crawled everywhere. They established a daily clean-up routine and gradually grew accustomed to their surroundings.

On the first visiting day, Mrs. Nehru arrived, although there was no car to bring her. Both her son's and Ranjit's car had been confiscated to pay the fines they refused to pay. She called a tonga, a two-wheeled horse-drawn vehicle, and jogged down the road to the prison.

After three very trying weeks, the trials were held, not in a law court but in the prison, where the "politicos," as they were called, were lined up against the office wall. The Nehru sisters had de-

cided to do as their brother always did, take no part in the trial
and have no one plead for them. Mrs. Pandit was called first. She
stepped forward. The magistrate pronounced her sentence:
"Vijaya Lakshmi Pandit, you are hereby sentenced to one year
of rigorous imprisonment and a fine of . . ." The magistrate's
voice was so low that no one could hear the amount, but it did
not matter. Mrs. Pandit had no intention of paying the fine any-
way.

Nan's mother and friends were stunned. They had expected
that she would receive a sentence of several months but not a
year. Everyone knew what an ordeal this length of time away from
her children would be for her.

The sergeant at arms next called Krishna Nehru, who stepped
forward to be sentenced to one year of rigorous imprisonment.
No fine was attached. The terms for the remaining political prisoners ranged from three to nine months. Only two others were
given a year's sentence.

On the next visiting day, when Mrs. Nehru arrived at the gate,
the guard gruffly announced, "They are not here. Your daughters
are gone."

"Gone where? Where are my daughters?" she asked in dismay.

"I don't know. Ask the chief," the guard replied and turned
away.

With difficulty, Mrs. Nehru learned that the previous night her
daughters had been taken to Lucknow. "You can find out the
Lucknow visiting days," the official said, "by writing the Superintendent of Prisons in Delhi."

It was the cold season in the United Provinces. Nan and
Krishna shivered as they packed their bags. At 10:30 P.M., they
had been awakened and told to be ready to leave at 11 P.M. At
the stroke of the town-hall clock in the distance, the matron and
guards came to their cell. A prison car took them to the railway
station, where, with eight other women, they were hustled into
the waiting train. The compartment was not heated; they had no

bedding or shawls and huddled together to keep warm. Before sunrise, the train stopped, the door was unlocked, and they were ordered out and escorted down the station platform into a prison van. In spite of the darkness, they recognized the Lucknow station, where often they had come, usually to be met and garlanded by friends. Now they bumped down the road to a building surrounded by high, bleak gray walls. Iron gates opened to receive them. The usual registration and inspection were followed by instructions from the matron. In a bored voice she said, "Five P.M. to 5 A.M. are the hours that you will be locked in your cells." Then she added, "Plan your day accordingly."

Nan and Krishna settled themselves as best they could in the new quarters. There was one improvement—there were no bugs or crawling things as at the Naini Jail. Their first concern was to let their mother know where they were, but they learned, when they asked about sending a message, that only one letter was permitted every two weeks. To their surprise, on the first visiting day their mother appeared. She had made the six-hour train journey alone. She brought news of the family and also word that an estimated eighty thousand Congress party workers had been arrested in the last four months and that, with the men in prison, in many places it was now the women who were taking the lead in Congress work. Many of them were women who had never before done anything outside of their homes. Gandhi had always believed that women should play as much of a part in India's struggle for freedom as the men. Now they were doing so.

Through the months, Mrs. Nehru shuttled back and forth from Allahabad to Lucknow and Bareilly in order to visit her daughters, Jawaharlal, and Ranjit. The trainmen came to know the tiny lady in a white khadi sari, usually carrying a bunch of flowers. Her visits not only brought joy and news to her children but also gave them a feeling of pride in their mother's courage. The months were difficult for the Nehru sisters, for there were no doors to shut out the cold when the chilly days came, and they longed for the hot months. Then when the summer heat arrived, the hot winds and the dust storms made life almost unbearable. But somehow they survived.

In early April, 1932, the political prisoners decorated their barracks and held meetings to celebrate National Week in spite of the disapproval of the prison authorities. A disturbing rumor reached Nan Pandit that Mrs. Nehru had been injured in the Allahabad demonstration. How or where the Nehru sisters could not learn until visiting day. Then they heard the story.

Their aunt, Bibi Amma, had begged her sister not to go to the celebration because the heat was intense, there was no one to go with her, and there might be trouble, as the police had banned such gatherings. Nevertheless, Mrs. Nehru went. At the hour for the procession to start, she walked quietly to the corner where people were assembling and took her place where she knew a Nehru should be, at the head of the parade. Soon the procession was on its way down the road, waving flags, singing, and chanting Congress songs. After a short distance, the police stopped them and ordered the crowd to disperse. The front line stood its ground, and a throng of people massed behind it. Someone from a nearby house brought a chair, put it in the middle of the road, and begged Mrs. Nehru to sit down. At first she refused, but as the heat increased and she felt tired, she did so.

The small figure dressed in khadi, seated in front of the milling crowd on the dusty road, did not know what happened after that. It all came too fast. The police charged; the marchers fled in all directions. Onlookers later said that Mrs. Nehru was knocked down and struck with a cane. She lost consciousness. When she came to, she was by the side of the road and everyone had gone; her head was bleeding and it ached. She could not get up, and once again she sank into unconsciousness.

Sometime later, a British officer drove slowly down the road to check the results of the charge. To his amazement, he saw a small crumpled figure lying by the roadside. He stopped his car, went to see what had happened, and was shocked to recognize the widow of Motilal Nehru. Gently he picked her up, climbed back

into the car, and told the chauffeur to drive to Anand Bhawan.
At once the servants ran to get Bibi Amma. The officer carried
Mrs. Nehru to her room and called a doctor immediately.

The news spread quickly. There were rumors that Swarup Rani
Nehru was seriously injured; that she was bleeding to death; that
she had been knocked down by the police and was dying. The
crowd in the bazaar went mad. They forgot Gandhi and his teach-
ing of nonviolence. There was but one thought—the British Raj
had struck down the mother of their beloved Jawaharlal Nehru.
Revenge was all that mattered. The crowd attacked the police.
The police fired. Several people were killed.

Finally word came that Mrs. Nehru was not dead, only injured.
Slowly the crowd grew calmer. Eventually they disbursed and
drifted to their homes.

When Mrs. Nehru was again able to journey to Lucknow to see
her daughters, the bandages were gone. She was unusually gay
and told the story to Nan and Krishna as though it were a minor
happening. "Just an ordinary lathi charge," she said. Yet her
daughters felt she was not as well as previously and were disturbed about her.

The prison days dragged wearily by for the Nehru sisters. The
monotony was the hardest thing to endure. The highlights were
the days when visitors or letters arrived and when the fortnightly
letters could be sent. Eventually the days became weeks and the
weeks slowly became months, which they checked off on the calendar Krishna had put up on the wall.

The sisters came to know their fellow inmates well. A few grew
more trying as the days went by; others, even some with criminal
records, they came to admire when they learned their stories. One
day Krishna said, "Nan, do you sometimes wonder what we might
be like if we had been brought up as they have been?" for many
of the prisoners had known nothing all their lives but poverty,
neglect, or cruelty.

Eleven months had passed when one evening, the end of December, the matron came to the barrack to inform Mrs. Pandit and Krishna that they were to be ready to leave at nine o'clock the next morning. They were speechless. The order read: "Time off for good behavior."

There were many farewells, some tearful ones. Their friends among the inmates were loathe to see them go. A strange comradeship had grown up since the law had brought them together and made them daily associates. "What do you suppose is ahead for them?" Krishna said as the gates swung open and she and Nan stepped out of the prison yard.

The matron took the Nehru sisters to Allahabad, where she turned them over to the police. Formalities completed, they were free. A tonga was called, and the sisters got into it. "To Anand Bhawan!" they both said at once. It was good to give this order again. They thought of what a surprise their arrival would be for their mother.

The tonga drew up at the gate. The old chowkidar, amazed to see them, threw the gates open and hurried to call the bearer. They dismissed the tonga, then looked about in amazement. The grass was dried up, the garden uncared for, and weeds were everywhere. Driveways were unkempt; trash had blown in and caught against walls and bushes. There was an air of desolation, and the house was strangely empty and silent.

The bearer came hurrying down the steps to welcome them. "Where is Mother?" they asked.

Two weeks before, they were told, she had gone to Calcutta with Kamala, who was not well.

The Nehru daughters felt utterly forlorn. To return home and have no one to greet them made them almost more lonely than they had been in prison.

"Come, Krishna," Nan finally said. "We are home. This is Anand Bhawan. We must get it into order again."

The bearer saw them looking at the unswept veranda, the dusty furniture, and the general disorder. He explained that their mother had let the servants go. There was no money to pay them.

As they went through the drawing room, they looked at the bare floor and asked where the large Persian rug was.

"The police came," the bearer replied. "They took it on the street and sold it. They said it was to pay the fine." Then he added sorrowfully, "The police came many times to take things. We could do nothing. Always, they said it was to pay a fine."

As the Nehru sisters went from room to room, they realized how much was gone. Many of the most expensive pieces of furniture and bric-a-brac were missing. For the moment, however, losses were forgotten as people began to arrive. Someone had seen them jog by in the tonga and had called friends. Soon the house was filled, and people kept coming until midnight. It was the first time in almost a year that there had been no five o'clock lock-up.

The bearer hunted up the old servants. The *mali*, or gardener, went to work on the garden; the faithful cook who had been with the family for years returned.

Eager to see their mother, Mrs. Pandit gave instructions as to what should be done while they were away, and the sisters left for Calcutta. A week later, the doctors decided Kamala was well enough to travel, so they all returned to Allahabad.

◈ 8

◈ MRS. PANDIT ELECTED TO
POLITICAL OFFICE

Ranjit Pandit had been transferred from the prison at Allahabad. Nan was most anxious to see him but decided she must first go to Poona to see the children. Krishna, who was suffering from malaria contracted in prison, went with her sister in the hope that the change would do her good.

To Mrs. Pandit the trip seemed endless, so eager was she to see her three little girls. Finally the train pulled into the Poona station. She hung out of the compartment window. The children, their cousin Indira with them, saw their mother and came running down the platform, calling, "Mummie, Mummie!" almost dropping their garlands in their excitement.

The train stopped. Mrs. Pandit pushed the compartment door open and jumped out. The children dashed into her arms, smothering her with kisses as she tried to stretch her arms around all of them at once.

During the days in Poona, the Nehru sisters were permitted several interviews with Gandhi, who was in prison there. The first visit was a very moving one. They tried not to show how shocked they were by his appearance, for two fasts had taken much of his strength. As a result of the ordeals, however, he had won his points with the government.

After a week of celebration in Bombay, the children returned to school in Poona. It was difficult to say good-by, but their mother told them it would not be long until she would come to take them home, and in May they would all go to Mussoorie for a holiday.

"Nan, will you tell Jawaharlal the news?" Krishna said one day after their return to Anand Bhawan. "I want him to know, but I don't know how to tell him."

The recent weeks had been exciting ones for Krishna. She was in love and hoped the family would approve of her marriage to a young man, Raja Hutheesing, whom she had met in Bombay. The romance began at a party given by a friend. Krishna had promised to send the new acquaintance a couple of her brother's books, for Jawaharlal could not use them while he was a prison guest of the British Raj. Later they met again when Krishna went to visit friends near Bombay. In her book that she wrote in 1944 called *With No Regrets*, she tells how, shortly before she was to return home, as they sat on a veranda, Raja leaned over and amazed her by saying rather casually, "When shall we get married, my dear?"

The next day, Krishna was suddenly called home by the illness of her mother. After the crisis had passed, she told her story to Nan and asked her to break the news to their brother, who had been released from prison because of his mother's illness.

Nan did so and later, on a visit to Bombay, Jawaharlal met Raja and learned that Gandhi knew the Hutheesing family. When Raja came to visit the Nehrus in Allahabad, Mrs. Nehru gave her approval to the marriage and asked that the wedding date be set as soon as possible, for she was fearful prison might again claim Jawaharlal.

On October 20, 1933, a small group gathered in the drawing room at Anand Bhawan for a very different wedding from that of Swarup's twelve years before. As Mrs. Nehru's strength was limited, the celebration was simple. It was decided that, since Raja was a Gujarati and Krishna a Kashmiri, there should be a civil ceremony for which only registration was necessary. As this was over in a few minutes, some of the older guests did not believe the couple was really married. One friend of the bride's father was heard to ask, in a puzzled voice, "When is the wedding going to take place?"

A few days later, relatives and friends gathered at the railroad station to see the couple off. As they stood on the platform, garlanded with flowers, they were in decided contrast to the previous departure of the Nehru sisters from the same place, at the same hour, accompanied by the jail matron. Now Krishna was leaving her childhood home and Allahabad for a new home in Bombay.

It was strange at Anand Bhawan without Krishna. Her mother especially missed her. Nan was busy with her three girls and Congress party work, and Kamala was far from well. The family was concerned about her, but she would not spare herself if her husband needed her or wanted her to go with him.

Since his father's death, Jawaharlal, although the head of the family, had paid little attention to finances. Now he discovered he must give more thought to money matters, for he and Nan did not want their mother to be without the comforts she was accustomed to. They decided to sell more of the remaining but unnecessary furniture and household decorations of Anand Bhawan. Consequently, Nan Pandit had to watch many things she had lived with since childhood being loaded on carts and driven away.

Nineteen thirty-four brought difficult days for Nan Pandit. Her mother was frail, Kamala's health was deteriorating, prison conditions were trying for Ranjit and also for her brother, who had again been arrested and taken to Calcutta. After a time, to her relief, Jawaharlal was transferred to the Dehra Dun Jail in a cooler climate and with a view of the Himalayas, which always gave him a lift of spirit. Then, at the end of July, without a word of explanation, he was sent home to Allahabad. Here he learned to his surprise and distress that the temporary release was because of the serious condition of his wife's health. His arrival was a tonic for Kamala and the whole family, especially when Indira joined them from the Tagore school, Santiniketan, near Calcutta, where her parents had sent her.

Eleven days later a police car drove into Anand Bhawan, and the officer announced, "Time is up. Are you ready?" There were hurried farewells. One small comfort for the family was that Jawaharlal was not returned to Dehra Dun but was taken to the familiar Naini Jail in Allahabad. Daily bulletins about Kamala were promised, with visits to her twice a week. For a fortnight the bulletins came, then stopped. Often Nehru would be ready for the visit, and the day would pass with no explanation as to why he had not been sent to Anand Bhawan.

When the doctors decided to send Kamala to Bhowali in the hills, friends in England succeeded in bringing pressure to bear on the government so Jawaharlal was transferred to the Almora District Jail, nearer her. Although there were orders for weekly visits to Kamala, the prison authorities did not always find it convenient to send him.

In the meantime, Mrs. Nehru went to Bombay to be with Krishna when her first child was born. Shortly after Mrs. Nehru's arrival, Nan received a telegram saying that her mother had had a stroke. Immediately she and her aunt left for Bombay. A few days later, on February 1, 1935, Harsha Hutheesing was born. At last Mrs. Nehru had a grandson. As soon as her mother was well enough to travel, Nan took her back to Allahabad.

Two months later, Krishna, Raja, and the baby left the April heat of Bombay for a month with Kamala in the cool air of Bhowali. While there, the doctors advised that, since Kamala was no better, she be sent to Europe. At once plans were made for her and Indira to go. When the motorcar that was to take them to the railway station at the foot of the mountain disappeared in the distance, Krishna wondered what her brother's thoughts were as Kamala again went in search of health, a long separation the price they must pay. The voice of the officer who had brought her brother over for the farewell visit interrupted her thoughts. "Are you ready?" he said to Nehru. "If so, we will go."

For eight years the British Government worked on constitutional reforms for India. The document that resulted, known as the "1935 Government of India Act," gave more self-government to the country, although the final authority remained with Great Britain through the powers vested in the Viceroy and in the governors of the provinces, all of whom were British. The Congress party resented the provision that in the federal legislature, the Indian princes were given 40 per cent of the representation, although their states comprised only 24 per cent of the population of India. Also, these representatives of the princely states were not to be elected by the people but appointed by the princes. Consequently, because of these and various other provisions, many of India's leaders were dissatisfied with the act and felt it did not provide self-government for the country as a whole. Nehru called it a "slave" constitution. In spite of this, in 1935 Congress decided to present candidates for election under the provisions of the act.

In Allahabad, Vijaya Lakshmi Pandit had become an active member of the Congress party, and as a result she was required to do whatever the party might designate. When, in 1935, it was decided that she should run for election to the Municipal Board of Allahabad, she did so. She was elected and appointed Chairman of the Education Committee.

The work on this board brought Nan Pandit into contact with all sections of the city, particularly the poorer areas. She had known something of the poverty of the villages, for she had visited them, but only her picketing had made her vaguely aware of the struggle to exist that went on almost at her gate. The wretched homes and the emaciated bodies of the children deeply disturbed her. She requested the Municipal Board to give milk to the school children who needed it. But milk was expensive, and many of the board members did not feel it was necessary. So the Education Committee chairman, with her usual imaginative approach to any problem she had to solve, decided to do something unusual. Boxes were placed in the lanes near the schools labeled: "A Pice a Day for Children's Milk." A *pice* is the smallest of India's coins, its value a fraction of a cent. This came to be known as "The Pice Fund," and many subscribed to it. As a result, some of the neediest children received milk.

This experience taught Nan Pandit an important lesson. She came to realize that the difficulty in doing social work was not only lack of money but also the complete unconcern and utter indifference of many people for the needs of others. When one of the wealthy members of the Municipal Board said that he feared giving primary education might some day make these children into "our masters," Nan Pandit was furious. She thought of the small, crowded, dark rooms where children were struggling to learn to read and write and replied that, unless they did become equals, she was sure some day they would be masters.

In September, 1935, Mrs. Pandit learned that her brother might arrive any day in Allahabad, en route to the Black Forest in Germany. Kamala was not improving, and English friends had again been urging the government to release Jawaharlal Nehru so he might join his wife in Europe. Permission was granted, and he arrived at Anand Bhawan with one day in which to arrange his affairs and those of the Congress party. Four days later, he reached Badenweiler in Germany and Kamala. Every morning and every afternoon, he walked from his pension in a nearby village to the sanatorium. He was not able to talk much with her, for she had limited strength. When Kamala was somewhat better, they went to Lausanne, Switzerland, not far from where Indira was in school.

In the meantime, word had come that Jawaharlal Nehru had been elected Congress president for 1936. It pleased Kamala that, a second time, this honor had come to her husband. It was, however, disturbing for him as communications arrived in regard to Congress matters, and he realized how urgently he was needed in India. Nehru consulted the doctors, and it was decided that he could return to India for a brief visit. Only a few days later, the trip was postponed. Each day was more uncertain. Kamala seemed to be slipping away. Her husband and her daughter were with her when, early in the morning of the very day Nehru had planned to leave, Kamala quietly left them.

Father and daughter had a short time together in the beautiful town of Montreux. Then Indira returned to her Swiss school and Jawaharlal Nehru went back to India to take up his Congress duties again.

In 1935, Vijaya Lakshmi Pandit could carry on her Congress party work to only a limited degree, for the children were at an age when they needed more of her time. After a French-Swiss governess proved unsatisfactory, she and Ranjit decided to enroll the girls at Woodstock, in the hills near Mussoorie. The school had been established by an American mission board primarily for children of missionaries in India, but it admitted other children as well. Many of the Pandits' friends disapproved of this move. They felt British education was better for Indian children. One woman asked Mrs. Pandit if she wished her girls to learn hiking rather than arithmetic and dollars rather than rupees and shillings.

In spite of the critics, the Pandit girls went to Woodstock, with Anna Ornsholt, a new governess, to look after them in a house near the school. Tante Anna, as they called her, was an asset. She could be trusted to take excellent care of the girls, and under her instruction they learned to do more for themselves. She taught them to polish their shoes, mend their clothes, and make their beds. Anna Ornsholt was Danish and always stood erect. When the girls slouched, Tara always remembered how Tante Anna would say to them, "Sit up! Walk straight! How will India ever be free if you young people always sit hunched up?"

With her daughters in school, Mrs. Pandit was able to devote more time to her 1936 political campaign. The Congress party had asked her to run for election in the rural area of Kanpur, near Allahabad in the United Provinces, the U.P. The area was currently represented by Lady Srivastava, wife of the Minister of Education, who at that time was the only woman elected to the legislature. Many people felt that it was a mistake for Mrs. Pandit to run for election in a district where defeat was almost certain. They were sure Lady Srivastava would not give up easily. The Congress party, nevertheless, was convinced there was no one better equipped for this seat than the daughter of Motilal Nehru. Nan Pandit herself had no doubt of the outcome. Others might question, but she was determined that if she ran for election, she would win.

Although campaigning was a new experience, Mrs. Pandit found it stimulating. Her constituency of thirty thousand voters was largely rural, so she went by car and train, in bullock cart and on foot, touring the district. She distributed pamphlets and spoke at public meetings, where she always made a special appeal to the women. She urged them to vote and to persuade the men of their families to support the Congress candidates. Although the majority of the women could neither read nor write, they were quick to grasp what the various political parties stood for. To her surprise, Mrs. Pandit found that many village women were much more responsive and alert to political issues than those she approached in towns or cities.

Nan Pandit had had some contact with audiences while serving as chairman of the Education Committee in Allahabad. However, the first time she was asked to address a large group in the campaign, it was a trying experience. She felt she had nothing to say. Then something unexpected happened to her. She sensed that she had become one with the crowd and that all she needed to do was to be their voice, to speak for them. She did so. The people caught her spirit and became one with her. When she finished, they cheered and cheered her. Often, through the years of addressing innumerable gatherings, she was to know this sense of oneness with her audience and they with her. Perhaps because of this, Vijaya Lakshmi Pandit's best speeches were usually her unprepared ones, when she spoke extemporaneously and from her heart. At such times, words flowed forth in a torrent and she captivated everyone.

During the campaign, there was no money for electioneering expenses or for the transportation of voters to the polls on election day if they lived in remote areas. Mrs. Pandit reminded those who listened to her that they thought nothing of walking long distances on a pilgrimage to a shrine or a holy place. This election, she declared, was a pilgrimage, a political pilgrimage to which they must dedicate themselves. "On foot to vote" became a Congress slogan.

Ranjit Pandit was also a candidate for Jumna-par, a constituency across the river from Allahabad. On the return from campaign trips, he and Nan exchanged amusing, encouraging, and discouraging experiences. Indifference, they found, was their most baffling problem. It was hard to make people who were unimportant in their villages believe that their votes at the polls mattered.

When home for the holidays, the Pandit daughters were sometimes allowed to attend the political meetings, although their grandmother did not approve. She felt that dusty roads and crowds were not the places for children. The girls were delighted when they could go, and whenever anyone would listen to them, they would urge people to vote for their parents. Lekha, armed with a Congress flag, would assure them that her mother would be of help to them if she were elected.

With their grandmother, at Anand Bhawan, they eagerly awaited the election results. It was an exciting moment when word came that their mother had been elected and, shortly after, that their father had also defeated his rival. There was a ten-thousand majority, they learned later, for their mother.

Shortly before the new legislature was to convene, a telegram came for Vijaya Lakshmi Pandit from the Premier of the United Provinces. It was most unexpected and exciting because Pundit Pant asked permission to appoint her Minister of Health and Local Self-Government, which, he stated, would make her a member of his cabinet. Never before in India had the post of a minister been offered to a woman, and in 1937 few countries anywhere had appointed a woman to a post of such responsibility. Ranjit Pandit urged his wife to accept. He felt that with the children away at school she would have the time to give to it, and he knew she had the ability to do the work well.

Vijaya Lakshmi Pandit recognized that it was quite possible the position was offered to her because it was an exceedingly difficult one that few would be willing to accept. She saw in it the possibility of working on some of the problems she had become aware of as a member of the Municipal Board, where she had learned much about health conditions, especially of women and children. She replied to Pundit Pant that she would be pleased to accept if the Premier felt she could best serve her country this way. It was a difficult assignment, to try to improve health conditions in India's largest province, but not only did Nan Pandit like a hard job, but she also believed this was an opportunity to demonstrate what women might accomplish if given a chance.

On the morning of July 29, 1937, when His Excellency, the Governor of the United Provinces, opened the Legislative Assembly in Lucknow, the capital, the fourth member to be called to take the oath of office was "The Honorable Vijaya Lakshmi Pandit." She left her seat, went forward, signed the register, shook hands with the Governor, and returned to her place. A wider political career now began for the daughter of Motilal Nehru; a real task lay ahead for her.

The election of the Pandits to the Legislative Assembly meant a move from Allahabad to Lucknow, where, as a cabinet member, a house was allocated to Mrs. Pandit. As usual, she turned a rather ordinary house into a very homelike place, while the garden responded to Ranjit Pandit's love of flowers. Once the house was settled, Mrs. Pandit went to see her office. It would be a new experience to have one. At the Civil Secretariat building, an attendant showed her to the door marked "Minister of Health." He opened it, and she stepped into the room. Then she stopped. She was overcome by what she saw. The office looked like a second-hand furniture shop. There was a huge desk, a leather sofa, several bookcases, and a jumble of tables and chairs. The walls were apple green, the rug an ugly pink. It was awful!

Instinctively picking up her sari, Mrs. Pandit cautiously crossed the unswept floor to speak to a young man, who in a timid voice announced he was her "personal assistant." At once, she sent him to find the janitor, who under her supervision rearranged the furniture so the room looked more attractive. She knew she must have flowers, so she sent for a bowl from a shop across the street and asked that it be filled with flowers from the garden of the Secretariat. The janitor had survived the other changes, but her request for flowers was too much. He was horrified. "Madame," he said, "you can't have flowers here in the office. It's never been done!"

"Hasn't it?" the Minister of Health asked innocently. "Then it's time to have some, so I will go down and pick them myself." The thought of a cabinet minister with a pair of shears in her hand was more than the janitor could imagine. Hastily he left the room, to return soon with a bunch of lovely red roses. From that day on, whenever the Minister was in her office, flowers were also there.

While Mrs. Pandit was arranging the room, an armful of files was brought in and stacked on the desk, apparently intended for her. She selected the thinnest one, sat down, and began to read. After a few pages she found, to her surprise, that the subject matter was not too difficult to understand, especially after she became accustomed to the official phraseology. Soon she was really interested and, having always read rapidly, had gone through a number of documents when she was interrupted by a knock on the door. She looked up to see one of the tallest Englishmen she had ever encountered. He introduced himself as the Departmental Secretary and asked if he could do anything for her. She rose and from her diminutive five feet glanced up at him. He was more upsetting than the pink carpet had been!

Before long the new Minister had adjusted to the staff and they to her. It was a new experience for them to take orders from a woman, but in a short time she had won their confidence and respect and they gave her their full cooperation.

Quickly, the Minister of Health learned that "politics is the art of the possible." She set her goal always beyond what she expected to achieve but made concrete plans for what she believed the Legislative Assembly would approve. She worked to increase medical dispensaries, with the hope that there might be one within five miles of every village; she set up an anti-malaria campaign; she secured funds for a few demonstration playgrounds with small libraries attached; she struggled to arouse interest in nursing as a profession. Then, without warning, an exceedingly serious problem confronted the Minister of Health.

For centuries, a Kumbh Mela—a great fair—had been celebrated every twelve years at one of the sacred places on the Ganges. Hundreds of thousands of pilgrims come from all over India for purification by bathing in the sacred river. In 1938, the Kumbh Mela took place at Hardwar, located at the foot of the Himalaya Mountains, where the Ganges flows through a very narrow outlet onto the plains below. The usual enormous number of pilgrims came. Among them, without anyone's being aware of it, were individuals infected with cholera. On their way home, as they walked down the dusty roads and crowded into the third-class compartments of trains, they infected others. Cholera broke out everywhere. It spread from village to village. Hundreds died.

As soon as word of the epidemic reached the Minister of Health, she immediately mobilized her forces, increased the medical staff, and went to work to try to check the disease. She toured the province, going even to the worst areas. She encouraged the medical officers and tried to build up the morale of the families of the cholera victims. In some villages, the Minister found that so many had died that there were few left to cremate the dead. It was the first time a minister of health had ever gone personally to see the effects of an epidemic. Usually a subordinate was sent to prepare a report. Mrs. Pandit insisted that her deputy minister accompany her, being determined that her staff should have firsthand experience of the tragedy of such an event. Her tour made a deep impression upon the doctors and medical workers wherever she went.

Eventually the cholera subsided, but no sooner was it under control than there was the threat of a malaria epidemic. Fortunately, the rains came and the epidemic was averted. The Minister of Health decided to begin a public-health program at once to try to prevent the recurrence of such epidemics. To her distress, she found she had no energy left. At her husband's suggestion, she asked for a two-month leave of absence and joined her brother, then in London.

When British journalists learned that the first woman minister of India was in England, they besieged her. She was eager for the public to know what she was attempting to do and gladly presented her program to the press. She told them of her plans and her hopes for her department. To her keen disappointment and irritation, the stories that appeared usually concerned the beauty and charm of the Minister of Health. "Why can't they treat me as they would a man?" Mrs. Pandit often asked, as for the first time she faced the difficulties of publicity for a woman in public office . . . especially an unusually attractive one.

At the first session of the legislature after Mrs. Pandit's return to Lucknow, members commended her for the work done during the cholera epidemic. The Minister of Health expressed her appreciation of their remarks and praised the "magnificent efforts" of all the health officials. Then she said very forcefully, "I beg to suggest that those gentlemen who are so eloquent in the house tonight, when they go outside, use some of that eloquence to explain to the poor, ignorant, superstitious villagers how they should help themselves and so prevent epidemics and disease from sucking up the life of our nation."

Vijaya Lakshmi Pandit carried a second portfolio; hence all of her time could not be devoted to health problems. She was Minister of Local Self-Government as well.

Many years ago in India, there had been a village organization known as the *panchayat*, made up of elders selected by the villagers, whose responsibility was to settle disputes, see that justice was administered, and look after the general welfare of the village. An old book called *Nitisara*, written in the tenth century, tells of these village societies. They had extensive powers, and the members were highly respected. Women as well as men could serve on them. Land was distributed and taxes were collected by the panchayat. There was one interesting rule laid down—that near-relatives of members could not be appointed to a public office. If there were many complaints made against an official, he was dismissed, for, as the *Nitisara* wisely comments, "Who does not get intoxicated by drinking of the vanity of office!" Character, merit, and work were to be considered in making appointments.

Through centuries, these panchayats operated in the villages until the British took over India. Now Mrs. Pandit had a study made of how they had functioned. She decided to reintroduce them in as many of the villages of the United Provinces as possible, with whatever modifications and changes seemed advisable. After they were established, the Minister of Local Self-Government visited them whenever she could and was pleased to discover how little difficulty the villagers had in recognizing their natural leaders. She was impressed by the wisdom and judgment they displayed, even though many of the leaders could neither read nor write. If the Minister went to a village where a panchayat had been set up, instead of a governmental official receiving her, it was the head of the panchayat who always welcomed her with dignity and simplicity. These visits often became festive occasions. She was garlanded, the requests of the executive group were presented with much formality, and, in spite of their meager resources, a feast was usually prepared in her honor. Mrs. Pandit felt a deep satisfaction in this work and believed something of lasting value was being created. People were learning to manage their own affairs and were developing a sense of responsibility for the welfare of the village.

When the Minister made her reports to the Legislative Assembly, it was an asset that she was able to speak in Urdu or English as well as Hindi, the language of the province. Mrs. Pandit would switch from one language to another if she felt she was not being understood. On one occasion an old friend, Raja Maharaj Singh, said to the legislators that he "would like to congratulate the

Honorable Minister on the clear and vigorous speech which she made," and added, "I have known Mrs. Pandit since she was a child, and it gives me great pleasure to observe the ability with which she fills her high office and the grace with which she adorns it."

◈ 9
◈ FAMILY CHANGES

In January, 1938, there had been a family reunion for the Nehrus. Jawaharlal and Indira were at home, Nan and Ranjit had brought the girls from Lucknow to see their grandmother, and Krishna with her boys—for she now had two—had come from Bombay for her annual visit. The last evening, they all sat chatting until it was time to go to the station for the night train. A meeting of the Legislative Assembly made it necessary for the Pandits to return to Lucknow.

Mrs. Nehru had been unusually talkative at dinner. Later she was quieter and looked tired. At ten-thirty, Nan got up and crossed the room to say good-by to her mother. Her mother rose from her chair, put her arms around Nan, and collapsed without a sound. Jawaharlal rushed to her and carried the small figure to her room. The doctor came, told them it was a stroke, and said that there was little to do. They sat in their mother's room all night. As a rose glow appeared in the early-morning sky, her heart stopped. "She's gone," Jawaharlal whispered.

A little earlier, they had persuaded their aunt, Bibi Amma, to go to her room to rest. Nan and Jawaharlal went to tell her the sad news. At first she refused to believe it. Then she rallied her strength and began the necessary preparations. It was the last service she could render to her sister, whom she had loved and cherished for so long. When she had finished, the lines of age seemed to have disappeared from Mrs. Nehru's face and it had resumed its youthful loveliness. Dressed in an exquisite sari, with flowers in her hands, Swarup Rani Nehru looked beautiful.

Word spread quickly through the city. People and messages poured into Anand Bhawan. In the late morning, thousands followed the body to the Ganges, where, according to tradition, her son, the pride and joy of Mrs. Nehru's life, lighted her funeral pyre.

The daughters remained on the veranda until the funeral cortege was out of sight. Like a statue their aunt stood beside them, not shedding a tear. When the procession had disappeared, Bibi Amma went into the house and to her sister's room. Here Krishna found her, apparently sleeping. Later, when she had not stirred and they could not rouse her, they called the doctor. Like her sister, she had had a stroke. All night the family sat by her bedside, and almost exactly twenty-four hours after her sister's death, Bibi Amma's heart also stopped. Her expression was so calm and peaceful that they knew life had ended as she wanted it to end.

When her husband died, Bibi Amma had taken the widow's vow of *sanyas*, which required that at her death she be dressed in a simple saffron sari with no ornaments and that no elaborate funeral rites should be performed. Consequently, preparations were very simple. Bibi Amma had taken no part in the social life of the Nehrus; few of their friends knew her well. Her days had been filled with meditation and deeds of service. Most of the people who came to pay their respects were old or poor, ragged or infirm. They were people whom she had helped when they came for her advice or to beg at the gate. None were ever turned away. To them Bibi Amma was a saint. They revered her and now came humbly and devoutly to follow the family group to the sacred river. Here her nephew, Jawaharlal, again performed the last rites—this time for the beloved aunt to whom, from his childhood, he had gone for help and comfort.

Presiding at U.N. General Assembly, Dr. Nervo of Mexico speaking,
September 28, 1953. (*United Nations*)

Swarup Nehru, aged two, with brothe
Jawaharlal, aged thirteen. (*S. H. Dagg o
Allahabad*)

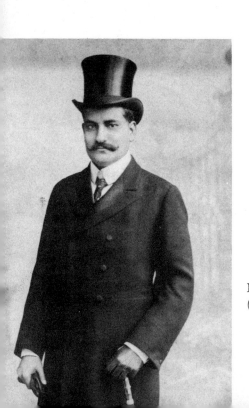

Nan Nehru at the age of six. (*Ju
Rust, India*)

Nan's father—Motilal Nehru, the law
(*Motilal Nehru Centenary Commit*

Nan Nehru with her younger sister, Krishna, 1914.

Anand Bhawan, the Nehru home. *(Press Information Bureau, Government of India)*

The Pandit family, in garden of Anand Bhawan, 1935. Back row, Mother, Father, Lekha; front row, Rita, Tara.

Pandit Motilal Nehru in
years. (Press Information Bur
Government of India)

The Minister of Health in the United Provinces, 1938.

Madame Pandit and her daughters meet the Romulos of the Philippines in 1947. Left to right: Tara, Lekha, Rita. *(United Nations)*

Madame Pandit with President Truman on the arrival of the Prime Minister in Washington, October, 1949. *(Acme Photo)*

Leader of the Indian delegation addressing the 1946 U.N. General Assembly at Flushing Meadows. *(United Nations)*

The Indian Embassy in Moscow.
(Jeannette Dale)

Madame Pandit presents two baby elephants, the gift of Prime Minister
Nehru, to the zoo in Washington, April
16, 1950. *(Wide World Photos)*

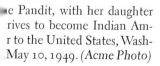

…e Pandit, with her daughter
…rives to become Indian Am-
…r to the United States, Wash-
…May 10, 1949. *(Acme Photo)*

Madame Pandit conversing with Secretary-General Trygve Lie, October 28, 1952, during the seventh session of the U. N. General Assembly. (United Nations)

Madame Pandit presents her credentials to President Miguel Aleman of Mexico in the Palacio Nacional, February 8, 1951. (Excelsior, Mexico D. F.)

Madame Pandit listening to the debate on the Korean question in the Political Committee, February 25, 1953. (*United Nations*)

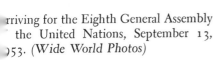
rriving for the Eighth General Assembly
the United Nations, September 13,
)53. (*Wide World Photos*)

Before the opening of the session at which Madame Pandit was elected President of the General Assembly, September 15, 1953. (United Nations)

Madame Pandit presides over the General Committee, considering the agenda of the Assembly session, September 16, 1953. (United Nations)

The President of the General Assembly with the Secretary-General, Dag Hammarskjöld, before the meeting of the General Committee, September 16, 1953. *(United Nations)*

Mrs. Roosevelt presents a gavel to the General Assembly President at the celebration of U.N. Day, October 24, 1953. *(United Nations)*

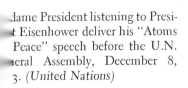

Madame President listening to President Eisenhower deliver his "Atoms Peace" speech before the U.N. General Assembly, December 8, 1953. *(United Nations)*

India House, London, office of the High Commissioner. (*Press Information Bureau, India House*)

Mrs. Pandit greets the Indian Finance Minister, Morarji Desai, on arrival at London Airport, August 29, 1958. (*The Times, London*)

the library of the residence of the
High Commissioner at 9 Kensing-
ton Palace Gardens. (*J. Allan Cash*
London)

The High Commissioner at her desk in India House. On the wall, a
photographic reproduction of a statue of the Buddha in the Gandhara
School. (*J. Allan Cash of London*)

The Ambassador arriving at the Roy
Palace to present her credentials to Ge
eralissimo Franco, Madrid, October 3
1958. (*Contreras, Madrid*)

The Queen Mother, Chancellor of the
University of London, confers an honorary degree on Mrs. Pandit, November
24, 1955. (*United Press Photo*)

Mrs. Pandit with one of her eight grand-children, Manjarai (called Manju), in the garden of her official residence, London, September, 1957. (*J. Allan Cash of London*)

Eamon de Valera, the President of Eire, with India's Ambassador to the Irish Republic on her farewell visit in 1961, accompanied by Miss Naidu, Governor of West Bengal. (*Irish Press*)

Her Majesty, Queen Elizabeth, and Prince Philip, assisted by Mrs. Pandit, place a wreath on the Samadhi of Mahatma Gandhi at Rajghat, January 21, 1961. (*Information Service of India*)

Her Majesty, Queen Elizabeth, being received by Mrs. Pandit when she came to dine at the High Commissioner's residence, March 28, 1961. (*Planet News, Ltd.*)

A cloud had appeared on the world horizon. World War II had begun in Europe. It seemed remote to most people in India but not to the Pandits, who knew Europe well and what their friends in England were living through. In Britain, the chief concern of people was what would happen in the next day, or hour to their families, their homes, and their island. They did not realize what a critical time it was for India as well. The Congress party questioned why, if the British were willing to fight to the last man to keep an enemy from occupying their own island, their government could not understand India's determination to be free from an occupying power. People asked how India could be expected to believe that this was a war waged for democracy when they were not free. The Congress party demanded, as proof, that the British Government give India independence at once or at least set a definite date when freedom would be granted. It was an agonizing time. All the leaders of India, who loved and admired the English, were opposed to the Axis and hated dictatorships, but they wanted, first of all, a free India.

On September 3, 1939, without consultation with the country, the Viceroy of India, Lord Linlithgow, proclaimed India at war on the side of the Allies. The act was legal but unwise, for Congress party leaders had declared India would not participate in the conflict unless its right to independence was acknowledged. The Viceroy's decree aroused indignation. Congress party members were shocked. The Legislative Assembly of the United Provinces at once passed a resolution that stated: "This Assembly regrets that the British Government has made India a participant in the war between Great Britain and Germany, without the consent of the people of India."

Five days later, the Congress party's Working Committee held an emergency session and sent a statement to the Viceroy. "If war is to defend the status quo, imperialist possessions, colonies, vested interests and privileges, then," it declared, "India can have nothing to do with it. If, however, the issue is democracy and a world based on democracy, then India is intensely interested . . ." The reply received from the Viceroy was to the effect that after the war, His Majesty's Government would be willing to consult with India in regard to the future.

As a result of this vague reply, it was no surprise to the Pandits that the Congress party's Working Committee called on all Congress members in the provincial legislatures to resign within a month. The resignations of Ranjit Pandit and Vijaya Lakshmi Pandit, Minister of Health and Local Self-Government, were sent at once.

Out of office, there was no reason to remain in Lucknow, so the Pandits returned to Allahabad and to Anand Bhawan.

The direction of future Congress plans was put in the hands of Gandhi, who attempted to see the Viceroy. When his repeated requests were refused, he saw no other way than to launch a civil disobedience campaign, using a few carefully chosen leaders. The party members waited for the first selection. It was Vinoba Bhave, a scholarly man, deeply devoted to Gandhi. The second was Jawaharlal Nehru.

The government did not wait for Nehru to act. He was taken from a train when returning from a visit to Gandhi, tried in Gorakhpur Jail, and sentenced to four years of rigorous imprisonment. The Nehru family and all Congress party members were stunned by the sentence. Even in England, many individuals questioned such a heavy penalty. Soon the Pandits also knew what was ahead for them when the police came and took Ranjit.

Since her arrest was almost certain, Mrs. Pandit's immediate concern was to make plans for her daughters, who fortunately were home for the holidays. Lekha, the eldest, was now ready for college. Arrangements were made for her to attend Chand Bagh, a college in Lucknow established by the Methodist Church of the United States. It was known as Isabella Thoburn College. The college had a reputation for a high standard of work, so Mrs. Pandit felt satisfied to have Lekha there. For the younger girls, Tara and Rita, she and Ranjit had decided that it was wiser for them to remain at home with Tante Anna, so tutors were engaged for them.

Each day Mrs. Pandit worked on household details, fearful the police would come before she finished. It disturbed her that there never seemed to be time to talk quietly with the girls, so she decided to write each a letter. One night when the house was quiet, she sat at her desk and wrote far into the night. In these letters, she shared with her daughters her hopes and dreams for them and their country. To Rita she wrote most, for she was the youngest but not too young to understand. Her mother told her that she would be a "Satyagrahi," one who practices Satyagraha, like her father and her uncle and must "keep the flag flying over Anand Bhawan." The letter ended: "We want smiles and grit to win through in the fight which will mean freedom for us all and for this big, beautiful India of ours." To her surprise, however, several months went by and she was still free, though her husband was in prison.

Late in 1939, a special honor came to Mrs. Pandit when, at its meeting, the All India Women's Conference, the most important women's organization in India, elected her its national president for the 1940-1942 term of office. It was her responsibility to preside over the 1941 convention, which was to be an unusual session, for it would be the first time the conference had ever met in a small city. Cocanada in South India had been selected, and the city felt it was a great honor to be hostess to such a distinguished group of women, which would include Vijaya Lakshmi Pandit.

Plans were going ahead for the gathering when, to the consternation of the committee in charge of arrangements, word came that Mrs. Pandit had again been arrested and the length of her prison term was not known. What she had feared for some months had now happened. After four months, to the great relief of those in charge, she was released very shortly before the conference was to convene.

On the opening day, December 21, 1941, when Vijaya Lakshmi

Pandit called the convention to order, there was a standing ovation. It was not only a recognition of their president but also a
tribute to her as a symbol of the part Indian women were playing
in the struggle for freedom. During the sessions there was an opportunity for Mrs. Pandit to tell the women how it had been
possible to do social work even in jail. She had persuaded the authorities to let her use a storeroom as a nursery for the young children of the women convicts, usually imprisoned with their
mothers. One of the political prisoners had helped by painting
pictures on the walls; another had modeled clay toys. For the il-
literate women convicts, classes in Hindi and Urdu were organized. Occasionally, Mrs. Pandit told the All India Women's Conference members, she had been able to get the authorities, or
friends outside, to supply additional milk for the emaciated, un-
derfed children of the prisoners, many of whom had never in
their lives had sufficient nutritious food.

There were discussions at the All India Women's Conference
about the way people reacted as political prisoners. Mrs. Pandit explained that not everyone was able to endure the rigors of
prison life, for it required moral courage. She had found that
those who really understood and accepted Gandhi's nonviolent
philosophy were able to carry on and even to develop and ma-
ture spiritually.

The convention, under the leadership of Vijaya Lakshmi Pandit, was an effective one. The members returned home with new
vision, renewed faith in the cause, and greater determination to
work for the betterment of their own communities and the freedom of their country.

Once again in Allahabad, there was much excitement at Anand
Bhawan. Mrs. Pandit's niece, Indira Nehru, was to marry Feroze
Gandhi. They had known each other casually in India and
then had met again when both were studying in Europe. It was
pure coincidence that Feroze had the same name as Gandhi, the
beloved friend of the Nehrus. Gandhi was Hindu; Feroze was

Parsi, a member of the Zoroastrian sect. In the eighth century, the Parsis first came to India from Persia to escape persecution. The majority lived in Bombay Province and were usually very successful businessmen or industrialists. When they arrived in India, the women adopted the Indian sari but wore it draped in a slightly different fashion from the Hindus so they could be recognized as Parsi.

After consultation with the astrologers, a March day was selected for the wedding. In order to help Nan Pandit with wedding arrangements, Krishna came from Bombay with her two boys. Harsha was seven, and Ajit, who had been born three days after the death of Kamala, was now six. The sisters were anxious to make the occasion a happy one, for it was inevitable that it would be a day when both Indira and her father would feel deeply the absence of Kamala. They were all thankful that after serving a little more than a year of his four-year sentence, Jawaharlal Nehru had been released and would be able to give away his daughter.

The wedding day was a bright and beautiful one. Anand Bhawan was overflowing with relatives and friends. The traditional Kashmiri ceremony, somewhat simplified and shortened, was used. For the Pandit daughters it was the first wedding in which they had had a part. Ranjit Pandit, who had been released at the same time as Jawaharlal Nehru, explained to his daughters the significance of the ceremony and reminded them that it was in this same compound that he and their mother had taken their "Seven Steps" together. He told them that the *Kanya Dan*, or giving away of the bride, was the most impressive moment, since it was a sacrificial act for a Hindu father to give away his most precious possession—his daughter.

After her friends had helped her dress, Indira looked exquisite in a sari made of khadi woven by her father during his days in prison. It had been dyed a pale pink and edged with delicate silver embroidery. Jawaharlal Nehru proudly escorted his daughter to the low cushion next to him. On the other side, the cushion where Kamala would have sat was vacant. When the ritual was over, Indira's friends rushed forward to shower her with flower petals and to sing the ancient song that calls upon a bride in her married life to follow the noble traditions of Indian women throughout the ages. Hindus believe that marriage is more than love between a man and a woman; it is also the link between the generations of the past and the generations yet to come.

The wedding festivities over, Indira and Feroze settled in a small house a short distance from Anand Bhawan. Their days there were few, for six months later the little house was empty. They were both political prisoners behind bars.

The hot season began shortly after the wedding and the Pandit family left for Khali, their mountain home. They traveled by train to Kathgodam, then by car up the winding, twisting road through evergreen forests to Almora and ten miles farther on to Khali. On the wide verandas they could drink in the cool, refreshing air and feast on the view, for Khali was at an elevation of six thousand feet. The house was on a knoll, where they could look out over the valley and up to the high Himalayas that surrounded it. Here Ranjit Pandit loved to come for refreshment and to work on his translations from the ancient Sanskrit. Ranjit had named the house "Ritūsamhara," which means "the gathering of the seasons." He selected the name so visitors might know they were welcome in all seasons of the year.

The hills were covered with wild flowers—violets, daisies, and orchids. There were raspberries, strawberries, and mulberries to pick, chicken eggs to gather, and honey to collect. As it ripened, there were quantities of fruit—pears, plums, grapes, figs, peaches, and cherries. Supper might be served on the veranda so they could watch the sun set and the white snows of the Himalayas turn to rose, then fade into black. If the evening was cool, pine cones could be gathered and a fire built in the living-room fireplace, where the girls might stretch out on the hearth rug to read or be read to. Their father often read portions of his translations or their mother her favorite verses from the "Bhagavad Gita" or some other ancient poem or story.

After a couple of weeks Lekha joined a party of her cousins and friends for a fortnight's trek to Pindari Glacier, and Tara and Rita went down the ten miles to Almora to attend a school of the dance recently established by the famous dancer, Uday Shankar. The weeks passed; the monsoon came; the rain fell. It would soon be time for the girls to go back to school. When they left, no one dreamed it would be the last time they would all be together at Khali.

◈ 10
◈ A THIRD PRISON TERM

In 1942 there was concern over the possibility of a Japanese invasion of India. The Congress leaders were uncertain and divided as to what should be done, yet they realized that inaction would be disastrous for the cause of independence as well as for the British war effort. Gandhi was determined, no matter what happened, to maintain his nonviolent policy. Yet he felt there must be something dramatic to rally the people. In a speech he stated that it was time for the British Government to "quit India," so an independent nation might mobilize its forces against the Japanese danger.

Shortly after, on August 7, at the meeting of the All-India Congress committee in Bombay, a resolution was passed calling on the British to quit India at once. The resolution stated that as soon as there was a declaration of independence, a provisional government would be formed and free India would become an ally in the war effort. But Churchill the year before had declared that he had not become His Majesty's Prime Minister "to preside over the liquidation of the British Empire." He was unwilling to make concessions. Soon after, people awoke one morning to see painted or scrawled on walls and sidewalks—"QUIT INDIA." Overnight the two words had become a national slogan.

The government reacted at once. On August 9, Gandhi and the members of the Working Committee were arrested. At five in the morning, the police came to Krishna's home in Bombay and took her brother, Jawaharlal Nehru, and her husband, Raja Hutheesing. These arrests caused nationwide protests, meetings, and demonstrations, often led by students. Lathi charges and mass arrests followed, frequently with the police firing into the crowds and killing or injuring many. Immediately a campaign of sabotage broke out. It was the most serious defiance of the British Government since the Sepoy Mutiny in 1857, almost a hundred years before. Between August 9 and the end of November, over a thousand were killed and more than three thousand injured in what came to be known as the "August Disturbances." Gandhi was deeply concerned that the movement had become a violent one, but in prison there was nothing he could do.

August 11 had been an exhausting day for the Pandits. The girls went to bed early. Mrs. Pandit was utterly weary in mind and body, for in the afternoon there had been a student demonstration and the police had fired into the procession. She knew it would be a long time before she would forget the faces of the youths she had helped to pick up and send to hospital. Lekha was now home from college and an ardent supporter of the independence movement. Her mother was fearful of what the days ahead might be for her. Ranjit had not yet returned from the Congress meeting in Bombay, so the problem could not be discussed with him. Sleep came to her reluctantly, despite her weariness.

In the middle of the night, when all were asleep, there was a knock on Mrs. Pandit's door. She woke with a start. Bindu, the night watchman, was standing at the foot of her bed. The police, he said, had come and demanded to see her.

At once Nan Pandit got up, slipped into her dressing gown, went in the dark onto the balcony, and looked down. At the door below, she recognized the city magistrate and the deputy superintendent of police with a half-dozen officers. The grounds were filled with plain-clothes men; some had come onto the veranda. Dimly she could see a string of trucks lined up on the road outside. She dressed quickly and, as she started down the stairs, looked at her watch. It was exactly 2 A.M. She opened the front door and, paying no attention to the officials, ordered the other men off the veranda. Then she turned to the magistrate, who was visibly uncomfortable when he announced he had come with a warrant for her arrest.

"Why is it necessary," she asked in a frigid voice, "for so many armed men to come at this amazing hour to arrest one lone, unarmed woman?"

There was no answer. The only reply was to inform Mrs. Pandit that the house must be searched.

She flung the door wide open. "Go ahead. Search wherever you wish. I have nothing to hide." She turned and left them and went to awaken her niece, Indira, who, fortunately, had arrived from Bombay that evening.

Nan Pandit was stunned. She had written Gandhi that because of the girls she doubted whether she should take part in the disobedience movement at this time. He replied that they would talk it over when he came to Allahabad very shortly. He did not come. He was arrested. Now the government had settled the matter for her, for she too was under arrest.

Indira was stoic. Many times, since she was four years old, she had watched her father go to jail. The last time had been only a few days before in Bombay. She quietly listened to her aunt's instructions, then dressed quickly while Mrs. Pandit went to awaken her daughters and break the news to them. Although startled by the suddenness of it all, the older girls immediately grasped the situation, asked no needless questions, and set to work to help their mother gather up what she was permitted to take with her.

They went downstairs together and found that the servants had lined up in a little row to tell their mistress good-by. They were concerned about the men who were prowling around, opening drawers, looking into desks, scattering papers about.

In the hall her mother looked at Rita, her eyes still heavy with sleep. She looked so small, only twelve, that for a moment Mrs. Pandit's courage almost failed her. Tante Anna was no longer with them, and there was no one to look after her daughters except a woman so recently engaged that no one knew whether or not she would be equal to the situation.

As Mrs. Pandit bent over to kiss her youngest daughter, Rita looked up and said, "How wonderful, Mummie, to live in these days. I wish I could go to jail too." It gave her mother renewed courage when Rita added, "Remember, we'll be fighting the British outside, Mummie, while you are fighting them inside."

Tara, always ready for any dramatic situation, whispered to her mother, "Let's say good-by on the veranda. I want the police to see how we take these partings."

They went out together. Tara, with head held high, eyes bright, said in a clear, distinct voice, "Bye, bye, Mummie darling! We shall keep the flag flying!"

Lekha went down the steps with her mother and before a quick, impulsive hug of farewell said very soberly, "Darling, don't worry. I will look after the girls." They walked slowly to the gate, where armed men slipped out of the darkness, surrounded Mrs. Pandit, and took her to the first truck, driven by the district police. No one spoke. The atmosphere was tense, the night pitch black.

Nan Pandit knew the road well. Often she had gone over it to visit her husband, her father, and her brother. It was the third time she had been taken to this prison herself, but never before had she gone in the dead of night. It was most depressing—all the more so when, at the prison gate, they had to wait half an hour to be admitted.

Finally the outer door was unlocked and the matron came out, puffing and panting as Nan Pandit remembered she always did when the unexpected occurred. She led the way to the familiar barrack; Mrs. Pandit entered and the key was turned in the lock behind her. She looked about. There was no cot. Utterly exhausted, she spread her bedding on the floor and lay down. She looked at her watch. It was 3:45 A.M. Her head ached and she could not sleep, for she kept thinking of the girls. They were young; perhaps they would go off to sleep again, she thought. She was especially disturbed about Lekha. At dinner that night, as they had talked over the day's happenings, a note of bitterness had crept into Lekha's voice. Her mother had wondered what she could do to help her catch Gandhi's spirit and overcome any hatred she might feel. Since Vijaya Lakshmi Pandit was now behind bars herself, it was hard not to let bitterness creep into her own mind and heart. Yet Lekha had spoken wisely that evening when she had said, "Mummie, we can't think in terms of normal life any more. There is no going back for us. We must go on to the end, whatever it may be." At last Nan Pandit fell asleep.

On awakening, Mrs. Pandit's first thought was of the girls. Her head still ached, so she lay quiet until the sweeper woman ordered her up. There were no sanitary arrangements and there was no water. She went into the yard, washed her face under the bathing tap, and felt better after she had walked up and down for half an hour.

At seven the matron arrived and promised to send food rations and tea. They came at ten. Mrs. Pandit gathered twigs, made a small fire, and ate a simple meal. She read and slept a little, then decided she would start a diary. She felt it might be a help to jot down her thoughts.

At 6 P.M., just as the air began to feel cooler and more refreshing, the barrack was locked. Then to Mrs. Pandit's surprise, the matron returned and informed her the barrack was to be left open so she might sleep outside. She dragged the cot, which had been brought her, into the yard, stretched out, and looked up at the stars. About midnight, the rain came down in torrents. She dragged the cot in again.

In the morning when she awoke, Nan Pandit longed for a cup of tea, but no tea had been sent her. She was outraged, for her daily rations should have been delivered. She wrote a stinging communication to the superintendent. A few minutes after it had been delivered, the matron came hurrying in with tea. The rice and other rations were poor in quality and mixed with grit, dirt, and tiny pebbles, which Mrs. Pandit picked out and saved. She took keen delight in showing them to the doctor when he came for inspection.

At sunset, Mrs. Pandit confided to her diary that this was her homesick hour. She was thankful for her books, though at first it was hard to read with the prison noises all around her. There were complaints and quarrels; abuses were hurled back and forth, occasionally ending in fist fights. At times she shuddered as she heard the cries of boys being whipped in another section of the prison. Many youths were taking part in the Congress party movement. In order not to have to keep them in the overflowing jails, often they were lashed and sent home. Even the nights were full of sounds. But eventually, Nan Pandit learned to concentrate and shut out the noise enough to lose herself in a book. Rumors and gossip circulated regularly, but only occasional newspapers brought word from the outside world. She longed to hear about her brother and Gandhi and what was going on in India. She wondered where her husband was.

To her diary, Mrs. Pandit admitted that she often fretted about little things and lost her temper. It helped to storm at someone. When the superintendent asked her if the cane with a leather flap on it that he had sent her for a fly swatter had been useful, she replied, "Yes, it helps me release my feelings."

"Are you satisfied?" he asked one day.

She snapped back at him, "Would I be here in jail if I were?"

The world seemed black when word came that Mahadev Desai had died. Nan Pandit knew how difficult it would be for Gandhi to go on without his devoted secretary. She remembered vividly the day Mahadev had casually given her an article written by his brilliant and lovable friend. Now she had lived for twenty-one years with that friend. She did not know where Ranjit was, but she was sure that when her husband heard that Desai was gone, he too would remember.

In previous jail terms, Nan Pandit had learned a special jail skill—to be on the scene immediately whenever anyone was released in order to appropriate whatever might be left behind. In this way, she had gotten a small rickety table, which now served as a desk and a dining table. She put her cot by the iron grating, where she could look out into the yard. A glimpse of green grass was refreshing. Often at night, she sat beside the grating to watch the shifting clouds and see the stars come out. It quieted her to realize they were always the same and undisturbed. Sometimes a moonbeam would delight her as it stole quietly across her cell floor. Then, one day, the grating was boarded up.

It was cheering when a young friend, Purnima, was arrested and put in the cell with Mrs. Pandit. They talked far into the night, since Purnima brought news from outside.

Over two weeks had gone by when one morning, feeling unusually low in spirit, Mrs. Pandit made herself a cup of tea and settled down to try to read. Suddenly there was an exclamation from Purnima. Nan Pandit looked up. There stood the matron and behind her, laden with garlands, her face beaming, was Lekha. She paused in the entrance to announce in triumphant tones that at last she too had been arrested. Finally the great British Raj had taken notice of her.

"But why are you here?" her mother questioned. "Why were you arrested?"

"Oh, it's a wonderful story, Mummie! The police said I had removed some plates from the railroad track so as to wreck a train.

Isn't it grand? I wouldn't know what to remove if I wanted to, and my engineer friends tell me the plates are so heavy I couldn't lift them. But it's a marvelous story and here I am!" she exclaimed.

Lekha dropped down at her mother's feet to tell her tale, for she was eager to relate the whole affair. At nine o'clock the night before, the police had come, but the girls were off on a picnic. The police asked for Lekha Pandit. When told she was out, they produced a warrant to search the house. When they could not find her and she did not return, they finally went away. "Then, Mummie," she said, "at eight this morning, as we were eating breakfast, they came again. I was seething with excitement but was determined to appear very calm and casual. So, Mummie, I ate an extra piece of toast to make the police wait. I wanted them to know this arrest was of no special concern to me!"

As she listened, Mrs. Pandit realized how much Lekha had absorbed as she had watched the arrests of her father and mother, uncle and grandfather and to what a degree she had imitated all of them. The story over, Lekha unpacked her few belongings and settled in. It was a joy for her mother to have her there, for in their busy lives they had not had much time together. Now they had long conversations and time to read books and plays aloud. It was ironic that it was imprisonment that gave them time to share their thoughts with each other.

Many of the hours in jail were spent in a continual struggle for food rations. They asked for fruit and waited ten or twelve days for a few squashed bananas. They asked for coffee instead of tea, only to be told coffee was not mentioned in the jail manual, so government sanction was necessary to get it. Later the superintendent brought a tin of coffee but told Mrs. Pandit the rules did not permit it. She was indignant and informed him she wished no special favors, that the coffee could be returned. Angrily, she threw the can on the floor at his feet. Her outburst had its effect. She was officially informed that coffee might be purchased.

A few days later, Indira and Feroze were arrested. Indu, as she was known, was put in the barrack with her aunt and Lekha in Purnima's place. It was good to have the latest news, although Indu knew little about her father or her uncle and the word in regard to Gandhi was not good.

To have the girls with her helped Mrs. Pandit. Bits of the ceiling continued to fall, there were just as many mosquitoes and gnats as before, the white ants still ate into their fruit, an occasional bat was a night visitor, a thin poisonous snake stretched itself one evening along the wall outside their window, but none of these things mattered quite so much when together they could laugh them off.

Lekha and Indu had fun naming the various areas of the small barrack room in which they were imprisoned. Fortunately, the window grating was again open, so Lekha lived in Bien Venue, Indu in Chimborazo, Mrs. Pandit in Wall View, for she could think of nothing imaginative to name her share of the room. The girls gave names to everything; the beds, table, lantern were all labeled. Even the hair-oil bottle, which lost its top, became "Rupert, the Headless Earl." The old blue rug Mrs. Pandit had brought with her bedding made the center space into the Blue Drawing Room. She could rarely remember the names, but the girls used them continually.

An elegant party the girls planned, with Purnima the only guest, involved lengthy discussions of food and whether the menu should be written in English or French. They saved rations for the great event and polished the cutlery, which consisted of a fork each and a single knife between them.

Ranjit Pandit had not been well enough to return from Bombay when his wife was arrested. Later, to her relief, she heard that he was back with Tara and Rita at Anand Bhawan. Two days later, at six in the morning, he was arrested and brought to Naini Jail. She heard he was somewhere on the other side of the wall. Mrs. Pandit longed to see him. It helped when Ranjit was able to send cuttings from the prison garden he had started the year before and an occasional book, which they devoured eagerly. Finally it was arranged that she and Lekha might have a fortnightly interview.

Then, unexpectedly one morning, word came that in an hour Mrs. Pandit and her daughter would be permitted to have their first interview with Mr. Pandit. While they dressed, they tried to think of all the things they most wanted to discuss with him. Nan Pandit knew from experience that the hour allowed for an interview was often gone with half the things she had most wanted to talk about still unsaid. She confided to her journal that it made her feel as though a volcano inside of her was about to erupt—in fact it often did erupt.

October 24 was Rita's birthday. It was the third time in Rita's thirteen years that she and her mother had been separated on that occasion. Once Mrs. Pandit had been in London, once she had been in prison, and now she was again in jail. It was especially hard this year, for during this third prison term, the girls were not permitted to visit their mother or even to write her. Regulations were much more severe than formerly. Always, it had been hard for the daughters to see their mother in the dingy, airless prison, wearing ugly, coarse saris. They were accustomed to her in what Tara later described as "the ordered beauty" of their home, on the veranda arranging flowers or in the kitchen making good things for them to eat. They were accustomed to having visitors say, "Isn't your mother lovely!" Now everything around her was unlovely. The birthday was a hard day for all of them.

On her brother's birthday, November 14, Mrs. Pandit recorded that it seemed terrible, when the country so desperately needed Jawaharlal and her husband, that both were unable to be of service. She rebelled against the situation and felt it was absurd to keep human beings locked up. It solved no problems and only created new difficulties On days like this, when Nan Pandit relived her childhood and thought of the important part her brother had played in her life, she wrote in her diary that of the many good things fate had given her, without question the best of all was her brother. She felt that to have known and loved him was ample justification for having been born. Twenty years later in an issue of *Wisdom* dedicated to Jawaharlal Nehru, Mrs. Pandit wrote that he had often inspired her and from him she had learned much.

As 1942 ended, Mrs. Pandit wondered whether the new year would hold more of suffering and sorrow or, as she wrote in her diary, "a glimpse of the promised land." Her hope was that they might all face the future with courage and dignity. But on New Year's Day she was depressed and recorded that, it seemed to her, the world had shrunk into two groups: "those who suffer for an ideal and those who inflict the suffering."

On February 9, 1943, when Mrs. Pandit and Lekha had their fortnightly interview with Mr. Pandit, he told them that the next day Gandhi was to begin his twenty-one day fast. The men who were political prisoners planned to observe a sympathetic twenty-four-hour fast. The women "politicos" discussed this and decided to follow the men's example. All day they fasted and a few minutes before lock-up time gathered for a prayer meeting to end the day. All were deeply grateful when Gandhi survived the ordeal.

Shortly after, because of a complicated situation at home, the government granted Mrs. Pandit a few days' parole, which was extended to a month. During this time Lekha was released. This made it possible for her mother to discuss with her an idea that she and her husband had had for some time. They were eager to get their eldest daughter to the United States to study. They felt that a few years in a free country would stretch her horizon and help her to grow up without bitterness, which they knew would limit what she might achieve in the future. At first Lekha was unwilling to leave her friends and go where she would be unable to play a part in the national struggle. Finally, after much discussion, she agreed, and it was decided that Tara would go with her. Mrs. Pandit cabled friends to request that the girls be admitted to Wellesley College. She was relieved when the president of the college, Miss Mildred McAfee, cabled that the college would be "proud and pleased" to welcome her daughters.

Before they departed, the government authorities granted Lekha and Tara a half-hour interview with their father. The jail superintendent and several officials were present. Ranjit Pandit made it a gay occasion, singing and joking with them, giving them no advice except, "Do what you feel is right and have a wonderful time doing it." Then he added, "Buy up all Fifth Avenue!" When the half hour was over, it was almost unbearable for them to leave the father they loved so much: a man of charm, rare ability, and unusual talents, with a fascinating personality. They did not know, as they said good-by, that they would never see him again.

The days were so crowded with details of passports, money matters, clothes, and farewells that Mrs. Pandit had no time to think what it would mean to have her daughters on the other side of the world. As the train pulled out of the Allahabad station, suddenly America seemed very far away. She wondered why she had let them go. Then Lekha's last words came back to her: "We shall keep the flag flying, Mummie darling, wherever we are. Don't worry."

Her parole over, Mrs. Pandit returned to the prison barrack, where she was greeted so warmly it almost seemed like a homecoming. It was hard not to worry about the girls. The war was not over; many ships were still being sunk. A month later, by chance, Mrs. Pandit found in the prison a newspaper with an item from Melbourne, Australia, to the effect that the Pandit daughters had arrived there en route to the United States. It was a relief to know they were that far on their journey.

It was a cruel blow to Mrs. Pandit to learn that her husband might be transferred to Bareilly Central Jail. The fortnightly interviews had been a comfort, and it helped to know he was on the other side of the wall. What she most dreaded was the effect this change would have on Ranjit's health. Bareilly was the worst jail in the province. The air in the prison was polluted by smoke from nearby factories. When her husband had been there previously, he had been ill much of the time. Nan Pandit was fearful of what might happen to him were he transferred. However, shortly after this, he was sent there.

For several days Mrs. Pandit herself had been unable to get up. The doctor came, but she did not respond to treatment. The prison authorities grew concerned. On June 11, 1943, after ten months in jail, Vijaya Lakshmi Pandit was unconditionally released from Naini Jail on grounds of health.

◆ 11
◆ NO LONGER "HAND IN HAND"

Although Vijaya Lakshmi Pandit was released, her husband was still in prison. It was almost more difficult for her to have him in jail than to be there herself. She always said that Ranjit Pandit was "a child of the wide open spaces." She could look at the present situation, ugly as it was, more objectively than he could. Even though he loved India with a deep, almost passionate devotion and would not be separated from its struggle, prison was for him a terrible ordeal. He hated the waste of having people shut up and unable to do constructive work. Mrs. Pandit's hope was that her husband's tremendous will power would help to keep his body fit in spite of prison conditions. But the overcrowded jail, the poor food, the hot, dusty days, followed by the dampness of the monsoon season, were bad for him. Word reached Mrs. Pandit that her husband was not at all well. She was deeply concerned, for she knew there was no adequate medical care in the Bareilly Jail. Finally, the authorities realized that Mr. Pandit's condition was serious, and on October 8, 1943, a little over a year after his arrest, Ranjit Pandit was released, as his wife had been, "on grounds of health."

Ranjit went directly to Allahabad, only to find that Nan, having no idea that he might be freed, was in Calcutta working for the famine sufferers. There was a very serious rice situation in the province of Bengal, which had resulted in starvation for many people. Since, with release and fresh air, Mr. Pandit felt better, he sent word to his wife that he would go to Bombay to see friends and join her in Lucknow shortly. The visit in Bombay over, he decided to spend a few days in their mountain home.

While in prison, Ranjit often thought of Khali and wrote: "I long . . . to sense the abiding peace and beauty of the forests which are unaware of the agonies and convulsions of a continent." Another time he dreamt of "the sun-drenched Khali garden where the acacia and the mimosa distill their seasonal fragrance and spread their feathery greenness on the mountain air." Amid the noise and confusion of the prison, he wrote: "I long to be quiet in the living room of Ritŭsamhara at Khali, dimly lit at the hour of twilight by the orange flames of pine cones and cedar log." Now he could wander among the trees or relax on the wide verandas and recall the times when they had all been there together or when he had gone alone to work on Sanskrit translations. After a few days in Khali, even though his health was still uncertain, he returned to Lucknow, as he knew his wife would soon be there.

At first, the Pandits stayed with friends in Lucknow, but when Ranjit's health did not improve, they decided it would be wise for him to enter the hospital. Here he seemed fairly comfortable, and Mrs. Pandit and Rita, who was with her, were encouraged. But most unexpectedly, at five o'clock on the morning of January 14, 1944, the nurse called Mrs. Pandit to come immediately. In an hour her husband was gone. She was alone and desolate. Her two older daughters were in America, her sister in Bombay, her brother and Gandhi in prison. She was engulfed in utter loneliness when the door of the hospital room opened and Rita rushed into her arms. She clung to her youngest child, and their tears flowed together.

As quickly as possible, Indira and her husband arrived, and together they took Ranjit Pandit's body back to Allahabad. Everyone was shocked, for few knew that he had been seriously ill. Even Mrs. Pandit herself could not believe what had happened. She had been so sure that care, good food, and rest would restore her husband to health.

In Allahabad the news spread quickly. Relatives and friends went to Anand Bhawan to await the arrival of the motorcar bringing the family. About four-thirty, it drove through the gates, and within an hour close friends lifted the bier, draped in the tricolored flag of the Congress party, and lovingly carried it to the bank of the Ganges. That evening, Mrs. Pandit, still overcome by the swiftness of what had happened, read and reread the cable from Lekha and Tara in America: "Be brave, Mother. He can never die. He lives in us."

For days, messages came from leaders in both the political and cultural life of India. They were a comfort, but most of all Mrs. Pandit wished she might go to Gandhi, as she had done so often in times of crisis. But Gandhi was in prison. She waited longingly for his letter. Finally it arrived. He wrote, "People will come to console with you, but I shall not sorrow with you. How dare I pity you? One does not sorrow for the daughter of a courageous father, the sister of a courageous brother, the wife of a courageous husband. You will find your courage within yourself."

Vijaya Lakshmi Pandit knew she must go on. In the midst of her grief she thought of the children of the helpless famine refugees. After thirteen days of mourning, Rita went back to school and Mrs. Pandit returned to Calcutta to plunge again into the work of relieving the stricken areas. Homes were opened, food provided, and money secured for what was needed. She appealed to all India for help and organized the "Save the Indian Children Fund." The need was great. Many starving villagers poured into Calcutta, often to die on the streets. Nan Pandit gave every ounce of her strength to the work.

When the worst of the famine was over, Mrs. Pandit's one desire was to be with her daughters in America. She also thought it might be possible to secure funds if she told the people in the United States of India's plight. The problem was how to get there. Wartime transportation was difficult, and she had no money. As a widow without a son, Hindu law denied her any right to her husband's estate. Women were recognized only in relation to men. So Mrs. Pandit and her daughters were not entitled to share the Pandit family property. For her, it was a difficult and humiliating position. She had never before known what it was to be without resources.

While in Calcutta Mrs. Pandit had come to know Dr. Pao, the Chinese consul. He had met his wife, an American, when they were both studying at Columbia University. Mrs. Pao was interested in Mrs. Pandit and was able to prevail on General Stratemeyer, then stationed in India, to allow her to fly to New York on a United States Army plane. The Army men were concerned as to whether a small, exquisite-looking woman could stand the rigors of a long flight and the discomforts of a military craft. Nan Pandit thought of her prison days and assured them that she could.

One thing Mrs. Pandit felt she must do before she left India—she must see Gandhi. With her father and her husband gone, it was he who gave strength and comfort to her. She went to his ashram at Warda in central India, where he had been since his prison release. While there, she discussed with Gandhi the possibility of attending the San Francisco meeting, where the nations were to draw up a charter for a new world organization. They knew that those who went from India would be appointed by the British Government and would not really represent their country. Though Mrs. Pandit would be on the sidelines, it might be of value, Gandhi felt, to have someone there who knew the viewpoint of the Congress party and India's aspirations for complete independence.

The question of finance arose, and again Nan Pandit felt bitter that Hindu law prevented her from having the funds to which she felt she was entitled. She told Gandhi how she resented her galling position. He made no comment. After they had talked of many things, however, Gandhi asked her very quietly if she had made peace with her relatives. She replied that she had not quarreled with them, so there was no reason to do so.

"Isn't there?" Gandhi questioned, then turned and looked out of the window. A few minutes later he turned and smiled at her as he said, "You will go, Swarup, to say good-by to your husband's relatives before you leave. Courtesy and decency demand this, and in India," he added, "you know we still attach importance to these things."

Years later Nan Pandit remembered how she replied, "Not even to please you, Gandhiji, will I go."

He smiled again, for Gandhi loved Swarup like a daughter and he knew how much she had suffered. "No one," he said, "can harm you except yourself. But I see enough bitterness now in your heart to cause you injury unless you check it." He paused a moment, then added, "You are going to a far country because you are unhappy and want to escape. Can you escape from yourself?"

They sat silent for a few minutes, then Gandhi said, "Will you find happiness outside when there is bitterness in your heart? Think it over." She could not answer. She said good night and went to her room.

The next morning, Nan Pandit rose early for the sunrise prayers that began the day at the ashram. Devotions over, she and Gandhi walked back to the house together. "Gandhiji," she said, "as always you are right. I know I must not let bitterness grow within me as it has since Ranjit's death."

At home again in Allahabad, Mrs. Pandit made arrangements to meet her brother-in-law, told him of her plans, and asked for his good wishes for the journey. After seeing him, she realized that she was more at peace than she had been since Ranjit died.

A few days later, a great Army plane carried its human cargo across land and sea. For the men, it was a home coming; for Vijaya Lakshmi Pandit, it was the opening of a door into a new world and unknown adventures.

When the plane arrived, there was no one to meet Mrs. Pandit, for no one knew she was coming. An Army car delivered her to a New York hotel, where she registered, then rushed to a telephone. It seemed ages before the operator made connections with Wellesley College and she heard Lekha's voice.

"Mummie, where are you calling from?" her astonished daughter asked.

"New York!" was the quick response. Then mother and daughter both burst into tears.

The reunion at the college was a wonderful one. There was much to talk about and many people whom the girls wanted their mother to meet. It was a comfort that they could be together for the first anniversary of Ranjit Pandit's death.

As they talked of the future, Mrs. Pandit told her daughters that she did not know what she would do now that she was in America. But since the opportunity had come when she desperately needed something, she had taken advantage of it. Already, she said, she felt as though being in America had given her a new driving force, and she believed a way would open for her to be useful in America.

A chance to serve came more quickly than she anticipated. As soon as it was known that Mrs. Pandit was in the United States, she was nominated to head the Indian delegation to the annual conference of the Institute of Pacific Relations. It was held in January of 1945 in Hot Springs, Virginia. Each time she spoke, there were favorable news releases, which created interest in the woman from India, who at that time was little known in the United States.

The conference over, a lecture bureau asked if it might arrange a tour for her. Mrs. Pandit accepted, and her public career in the United States began. Through her lectures, she came to know

Americans and they to know and admire her. The publicity sent
out by the bureau announced that Vijaya Lakshmi Pandit was
one of the world's most important women, "notable for her great
ideals and deep personal sacrifices." It also predicted that she
would be even more widely known in the postwar years. Her most
popular lecture topics were "Why India Wants Independence"
and "What Kind of a Postwar World?"

People who heard Mrs. Pandit realized her devotion to her
country as shown through her twenty years of work with the
Indian National Congress party, her concern for the betterment
of mankind, and her conviction that only democratic institutions
and freedom of thought could win the peace and solve the enormous problems that would follow the war. News stories emphasized Mrs. Pandit's unusual knowlege of world affairs, her keen
mind and telling wit, her poise and her beauty. People who saw
her for the first time were often surprised that she wore almost no
jewelry. A ring and a wrist watch and, if the blouse required it, a
pin at her throat . . . that was all. To those who knew India
this seemed unique, for jewelry is so much a part of the costume
of Indian women that people expected to see earrings, a necklace,
and many bracelets, called bangles in India. When Nan Nehru
married, she had much beautiful jewelry, but after the Nehrus
became active in the independence movement, she wore only
khadi saris with which jewelry was never worn. When the wearing
of khadi was no longer necessary as a patriotic symbol, Mrs. Pandit's husband had recently died, and she, as a widow, had no desire to wear ornaments. Consequently, she gave her jewelry to her
daughters.

For a woman of Mrs. Pandit's natural beauty, however, ornaments were not needed to enhance her charm. People often commented on her lovely wavy hair, always simply but perfectly
groomed. She did choose her saris with care, frequently wearing a
gray that matched her hair or pastel shades. She looked exceptionally beautiful in a soft ashes of roses, blue, or lavender. For
formal occasions, Mrs. Pandit usually chose a black sari with or

without border according to the style of the year or the elegance of the function. In black, she was regal as she ascended official stairs carpeted with red velvet, sat at the head table at a banquet, or participated in other formal gatherings.

It was easy for newsmen to write an interesting story about such a fascinating woman of the East. As Mrs. Pandit went from city to city, pleading for understanding of her country with the spirit of a crusader, one paper labeled her lecture tour "a whirlwind which left people breathless."

The lecture tour not only made her known to America, but it also helped to solve the financial problem for her and for Rita, who had meanwhile arrived from India by boat. They found a New York apartment. In her book, Tara recounts how her mother told people it was just off Park Avenue, but Lekha, with her journalist's training, informed her friends it was opposite the Gay Nineties Cafe, while factual Rita said, "I tell my friends it's above a wine shop. But it is no ordinary wine shop, for it belongs to an earl."

One real disappointment resulted from the tour. When Mrs. Pandit finished a Los Angeles engagement, it was impossible to reach Wellesley in time for her daughter's graduation. Lekha's diploma was presented without her mother's having the joy of seeing her accept it. To make up for this misfortune, Mrs. Pandit decided that Lekha should have a twenty-first birthday party that she would never forget. It was to be a beautiful affair and, if necessary, an extravagant one—a dinner dance at the Waldorf-Astoria Hotel for Lekha and her friends. If it took every penny she had received from her lectures, Mrs. Pandit would pay the bill gladly.

The speaking tour was the first time in her life that Vijaya Lakshmi Pandit had earned money, and it did something for her that she felt was very important. All her life she had been accustomed to lavish living and, in her youth, to large expenditures for such things as trips abroad, motorcars, and expensive entertainment. Her father, however, had paid all the bills. She had no idea what anything cost. Later this luxurious period ended, but there was always comfortable living. During the prison terms, the few annas (equivalent to a few cents) Mrs. Pandit had to spend were doled out by the jail authorities. Alone after her husband's death, deprived by Hindu law of his assets, she was left with a feeling of great insecurity. She feared the future. But in the month of lecturing, an amazing change came about in her. She had lectured to thousands of people and had been paid for doing so. They had listened to her enthralled, and she had gained courage and a feeling of security. She felt she could now say to herself, "Whatever happens, I can face life. I can take care of myself and, if need be, my daughters as well."

When the wonderful birthday party at the Waldorf was over, Mrs. Pandit said to her girls, "Treasure your memories. They are your personal bank account and give you a bank balance." Then she added, "Events like tonight create a past to live with. Treasure this memory always."

It was an exciting moment when Vijaya Lakshmi Pandit wrote the first really large check she had ever written. It was made payable to the Waldorf-Astoria Hotel. Years later she said to a friend that no one could imagine what that party did for her after the years of living on the brink with prison guards and locked doors. "Though only a gay party," she said, "that evening gave me a sense of release." She smiled as she added, "What a joy it was! Even today I remember every detail, and I always will. A new world had opened. I was happier than I had been for years!"

◆ 12
◆ MRS. PANDIT AT THE
UNITED NATIONS CHARTER CONFERENCE

In the fall of 1945, the American papers were filled with news concerning the Charter Conference of the United Nations in progress in San Francisco. Mrs. Pandit was eager to be there. She knew that the Indians attending it, most of them friends of her father, had been selected by the British Government because they had remained loyal to the Crown and would not raise embarrassing questions. Mrs. Pandit was sure she could make the situation uncomfortable for them and was determined to do so.

She discovered, however, that to attend as an "observer" one must represent an organization. She was baffled but kept hoping for another miracle to happen, and it did. A member of the Committee for Indian Freedom suggested that Mrs. Pandit, so recently arrived from India, would be an excellent representative for their organization at the conference, and the India League asked to co-sponsor her. She accepted at once and, with the necessary credentials and funds, flew to San Francisco. Here she was met by a large group of Indians and, to the delight of the photographers, was garlanded in true Indian fashion. The next morning her picture was in all the San Francisco papers.

An unexpected problem, however, confronted her on arrival. Hotels were filled; all rooms were reserved for delegates. "Was Mrs. Pandit a delegate?" the hotel clerks asked. She had to reply she was not. "We are sorry. We can't help you." The reply was always the same. She was desperate. The first night she sat in a hotel lobby. The next morning a friend heard of her plight and shared her hotel suite with Mrs. Pandit until she could get a room.

Another problem arose as to how she could get India's case presented to the conference. Already the British Embassy in Washington was shocked by her campaigning for India, while in England a Tory paper labeled her "a nuisance." Mrs. Pandit decided to send a memorandum to the Secretary-General in the name of the organizations she represented, then immediately after to hold a news conference to inform the press of what she had done. Many sessions of the conference, while essential, were tedious, so when newsmen heard of a special press conference across the street in the Scottish Rites Auditorium, they flocked to it. "What a relief!" many exclaimed when they saw Vijaya Lakshmi Pandit.

The correspondents sent out story after story about the small, beautiful Indian woman who was defying the British Empire, championing the cause of the oppressed, and calling upon the nations to begin at once to live up to the noble phrases that were being written into the Charter. Mrs. Pandit's campaign, many agreed, was a brilliant piece of electioneering. They did not realize how many years of experience her work with the Congress party had given her, so were amazed at her daring. She seemed instinctively to know the strategic thing to do and the most effective moment to strike.

Few who heard her would ever forget the day when, aflame with the passion of her convictions, Vijaya Lakshmi Pandit read to the press the memorandum she had sent to the Secretary-General. Her voice was clear and strong as she said, "I speak here for my country because its voice has been stilled by British duress. But I speak also for those countries, which like India, cannot speak for themselves. The voice of six hundred million of the enslaved people of Asia may not be officially heard at this conference . . . but there will be no real peace on earth so long as they are denied justice."

Many invitations came for Mrs. Pandit to speak to various groups. She accepted whenever she could. The California legislature asked her to come to Sacramento and gave her a standing ovation when she finished. Five thousand people welcomed her in the Sikh Temple of Stockton, California, where she reminded her audience that the sons of India had perished on practically every battle front of World War II.

As she spoke, something seemed to break loose within Nan Pandit. The pent-up frustrations and restrictions of prison days were gone. She herself did not dream she could use such forceful words to express the thoughts that poured forth as though a dam had broken. She swayed her audiences, and almost always they broke into prolonged applause. Her passionate appeals for tolerance and understanding of India won her many sympathizers. Although the days were strenuous, Mrs. Pandit was amazed that nothing seemed too hard if it meant that she could get her message across. Each success gave her strength to go on to the next; each contact with a new group seemed to recharge the inner batteries that kept her going.

The news reports were unusual, often fantastic, as she was described as "dainty and deft, with the velocity of the wind . . . that rides roughshod over all obstacles." Also she was called "A daring robin that dashes in and steals the tidbit right from under the beak of some bigger, more ferocious bird."

Years afterwards, as she looked back on the San Francisco days, Mrs. Pandit said, "I had great fun! One can when one has no responsibility. I had none. I was aware I was stealing the show from the British-Indian delegates and loved doing it. In fact, I deliberately went out to do so whenever possible. But," she added, "I did not do it for myself. I did it for India."

Back in New York, Christmas of 1945 was a gay and happy time for the Pandits. They decorated their apartment, gave gifts, and had a real American Christmas, determined not to let the fact they would soon be separated mar their joy.

Mrs. Pandit had followed the elections in the United Kingdom with keen interest, for she knew if the Labour Party won, it would undoubtedly bring India nearer to independence. It was an important occasion for the Pandits when Sir Winston Churchill turned over the responsibilities of prime minister to Clement Attlee of the Labour Party. The new government announced that, within a few months, elections would be held for the central and the provincial legislatures of India. This meant that Mrs. Pandit must return to campaign for a seat in the Legislative Assembly of the United Provinces.

Consequently, after the holidays, Tara went to Wellesley, Rita to Putney School in Vermont, where she had been since shortly after her arrival, and plans were made for Lekha to leave for India in March. Then in early January, 1946, Mrs. Pandit flew home in order to play her part in the important developments that were now ahead for India.

Once more in Allahabad at Anand Bhawan, Mrs. Pandit learned that the choice of the next president of the Congress party was considered a most significant one. If an interim government came into being, the president of the party would probably be asked to form it. There were three candidates. Jawaharlal Nehru was one of them, and Gandhi's choice.

Mrs. Pandit's own constituency welcomed her home. They had followed her days in the United States with interest and pride. At once she plunged into the election campaign, this time unopposed. As she electioneered, she told her audiences of the writing of the United Nations Charter and her impressions of America. When the balloting was over, she had been elected by an unusually large vote.

On April 25, 1946, after the members of the Legislative Assembly were sworn in, the Honorable Mrs. Vijaya Lakshmi Pandit again became Minister of Health and Local Self-Government.

Nineteen forty-six was a tense year. In March the government in London sent to India a cabinet mission of three members who came to be known as "The Three Wise Men." This time they succeeded in convincing the Congress party that Great Britain was serious about India's independence. They returned to London, nevertheless, with little accomplished, for the struggle between the Moslem League and the Congress party had made plans difficult. Mr. Jinnah, leader of the Moslem League, had become increasingly determined that India should be divided and the Moslems have a country of their own to be called Pakistan.

In mid-May, Jawaharlal Nehru was unanimously elected president of the Congress party and, shortly after, the Viceroy, Lord Wavell, invited him to form an interim government for India. To many, it seemed almost unbelievable that after the years of struggle, the goal of independence had really been achieved. The Congress leaders, however, were not entirely happy about the situation, as the plan for turning over the government seemed complicated and cumbersome and few believed it would work. Also, people began to realize that in spite of Gandhi's and Nehru's determination to keep India united, it might be divided. There seemed to be no other way out.

◈ 13
◈ LEADER OF INDIA'S FIRST MISSION
   TO THE UNITED NATIONS

Frequently, the unexpected happened to Vijaya Lakshmi Pandit, but it was a surprise when the Viceroy, Lord Wavell, selected her to head the Indian delegation to the General Assembly of the United Nations, convening on October 23, 1946, in New York. Since India as yet had only an interim government, the appointment had to be confirmed by the British Government in London and her credentials sent from the Court of St. James's. This was done almost immediately and reservations made for Mrs. Pandit at a New York hotel. This time on arrival in the United States, she would not have to struggle to find a place to live.

In January of 1946, the First General Assembly of the United Nations was held in Central Hall, London, but the second half of the session was to be in the United States, the country selected for the permanent headquarters of the United Nations. Temporarily, it would meet in a building originally constructed for the New York World's Fair, in Flushing Meadows. Here the delegates from fifty-one member nations gathered. When Mrs. Pandit arrived, camera bulbs flashed and reporters pursued her, eager for a statement from the first and only woman to head a delegation. Among those present for the General Assembly were men she had come to know when she unofficially attended the Charter Conference in San Francisco. Now she met them on an equal footing, not only as a member but also as the leader of a delegation. It was an impressive occasion when at four o'clock on October 23, in the improvised Assembly Hall, she took her seat at the desk marked INDIA.

Two days later, at the afternoon session on October 25, after the Argentine delegate had finished speaking, the President of the Assembly, Paul-Henri Spaak of Belgium, said, "I now call upon Mrs. Pandit, representative of India." For the first time a woman rose from her seat, went down the aisle and to the speakers' dais to address the Assembly. To her it did not seem strange, for she had spoken often in the Legislative Council of her province, but to many it was an historic occasion.

Vijaya Lakshmi Pandit began: "I stand before this great Assembly—unique in the annals of human history—where representatives of freedom-loving countries of the world are gathered together, to proclaim not only the adherence of my country to the principles and purposes of the United Nations embodied in the Charter, but the determination of our people to help make it a reality." She admitted that India had yet to achieve complete independence, but her country was so far along the road to freedom that for the first time India's delegation to an international assembly had been briefed and accredited by a national government. She told the Assembly that the Minister of Foreign Affairs, Jawaharlal Nehru, had stated that India would participate fully in the varied activities of the United Nations and assume the role to which her geographic position, population, and contribution toward peaceful progress entitled her. The Indian delegate made it clear that her country stood for the independence of all colonial and dependent peoples and their full right to self-determination.

As Mrs. Pandit spoke to the Assembly, she was poised, dignified, and beautiful. She spoke eloquently and forcefully, reminding the delegates that India, as a major power, located in a strategic area, would play an important part in world economy and was entitled to a place in the important organs of the United Nations, especially the Security and Trusteeship Councils. Her country, she declared, was also entitled to an adequate share in the administration of the organization. Then she added, "Permit me to say a word expressing my hopes and those of my country about the greater participation of women in the work of the United Nations." She told them that Indian women were now taking part in all nation-building activities, that India believed responsibilities must be shared jointly by men and women in order to create a better and more balanced world.

The first speech of a woman in the Assembly ended with ringing words as Vijaya Lakshmi Pandit said, "Let us recognize that human emotions and needs of the world will not wait for an indefinite period. To this end let us direct our energies and, reminding ourselves that in our unity of purpose and action alone lies the hope of the world, let us march on."

The item on the Assembly agenda that especially concerned India was the treatment of Indians in South Africa, the problem that had been of concern to Gandhi many years before. For nearly a week there were prolonged sittings of the Joint Political and Legal Committees (the First and Sixth Committees) with almost a record number of delegates participating in the debate. It was a disappointment to Mrs. Pandit that the resolution passed by the joint committee and sent to the Assembly was not as strong as India wanted. It was a middle-course one, presented by France and Mexico, which called on South Africa and India to work together to reform the South African laws that discriminated against Indians and other racial groups.

In the General Assembly, Mrs. Pandit's chief opponent in the debate was the distinguished delegate from South Africa, General Jan Christiaan Smuts. They were friends, but now they crossed swords, since he contended this was a "domestic issue" and not the concern of the United Nations. As Mrs. Pandit pleaded her cause, it became not a domestic but a moral issue. "I ask no favor for India. . . . I ask for the verdict of this Assembly on a proven violation of the Charter. . . . Mine is an appeal to conscience, the conscience of the world which the United Nations Assembly is."

Delegates were amazed at the way she set forth her facts, at her persuasive skill and her sense of humor. As she made her points clearly and forcefully, many delegates were forced to ask themselves whether or not their countries had acted justly. As the debate drew to a close, in her final speech Mrs. Pandit said, "We have now come to the end of a long and protracted debate. . . . I want to express the gratitude, not only of the people of India and the Indians of South Africa, but of the millions in every country whose hearts have been warmed and whose minds are eased by this impressive expression of world opinion in defense of justice and fundamental human rights." She thanked the Assembly for what she felt amounted to a great act of faith, for "we shall remember that the oppressed have friends in every country and under every climate." She closed saying, "I left the question with your conscience yesterday. I am content to let it rest there today."

A long, time-consuming discussion followed as to whether a two-thirds vote was required for the resolution to pass or whether a simple majority was sufficient. When it was decided a two-thirds vote was needed, Mrs. Pandit was not certain of the outcome. The roll of the member nations was called, and the votes were counted. Then the President announced: "The result of the voting is as follows: members voting 47; in favor 32, against 15, abstentions 7. The two-thirds required is 32 votes. The proposition is therefore adopted by 32 votes." It was close, but it was a victory and a great moment for India and Vijaya Lakshmi Pandit.

Although the resolution was passed, it was in reality a hollow victory. South Africa refused to take action, and the situation for the Indians there did not improve. The debate, however, had had international coverage, which made people all over the world aware of the plight of the Indians in South Africa and also aware that oppressed people everywhere had a champion in Vijaya Lakshmi Pandit of India.

When the General Assembly session was over, Mrs. Pandit said good-by to Tara and Rita and left for India. It had been wonderful for them to have her in New York, and as often as possible they had gone with her to the sessions, which had given them an opportunity to see and often to meet the world leaders who were there. In India, another task now awaited Mrs. Pandit. She had been named a member of the assembly to draw up the constitution of the new India.

At the first session of the United Provinces legislature, which she attended after her return, the Honorable Speaker said: "Before I pass on to other work, I take this opportunity of offering our heartiest felicitations to the Honorable Member, Mrs. Vijaya Lakshmi Pandit, for the great work she has done for the country in America."

◆ 14

◆ MADAME AMBASSADOR TO
THE U.S.S.R.

The Ministry of External Affairs of India's interim government had important work to do. Relations had to be established with other countries and ambassadors appointed to represent India in the capitals of the world.

When it was announced that the Indian and Russian governments were to exchange diplomats, there was much speculation as to who would be sent. It must be a person of distinguished accomplishments, who would interpret the best of India to the U.S.S.R. Someone suggested that Vijaya Lakshmi Pandit had made a decided impression on international circles when, as head of the Indian delegation at the United Nations, she had vigorously opposed General Smuts in the debate in regard to Indians

in South Africa. The question was asked: "Why not do the unusual? Why not appoint a woman to be ambassador?"

After much discussion, the cabinet approved the idea, and Mrs.
Pandit was approached. She was surprised, for she knew little
about Russia. Few Indians had been there and no one officially.
She talked over the matter with her brother to learn whether he
believed this was the way she could best serve India at this time.
She found it difficult to think of being away when so many important changes were taking place in the country. In the end, it
was agreed that she should go, and word was sent to Moscow. An
immediate reply came that Madame Pandit would be most welcome.

Quickly the news spread, and to press inquiries Mrs. Pandit
answered that she was fully conscious of the significance of the
appointment and hoped that, while in Russia, she might create a
place for India in the diplomatic life of Moscow. Many friends
were skeptical and certain she would be lost in what seemed to
them to be "the vast wilderness of Russia." As the days passed,
Mrs. Pandit became increasingly interested in the assignment.
She always enjoyed a difficult job, liked adventure, and had no
fear of the unknown. To her delight, it was decided that Lekha,
who had studied journalism at Wellesley, should go with her
mother as press attaché.

At the end of July, the new ambassador left for Bombay and a
week filled with lectures and meetings, social events and interviews. The *Hindustan Times*, in reporting her visit, stated that
"if ever one woman could hold the scene, this little lady showed
she could." They reminded their readers that she had done so in
America and now would try to do the same thing in Russia,
"where men like Napoleon and Hitler got lost. Of course," the
paper added, "Mrs. Pandit is not going as an invader, so she may
conquer."

On August 5, 1947, the Ambassador to the U.S.S.R. climbed
into a gleaming new plane of Air India. Three days later, she

came down the steps of the first foreign plane (other than the private one of the American ambassador) to land on Soviet soil. U.S.S.R. officials, and the Commonwealth ambassadors with their wives, were waiting to greet her. Official courtesies over, the Acting Chief of Protocol presented her with a large bouquet of flowers, then escorted her to his car and to the hotel.

A week later, on August 13, Vijaya Lakshmi Pandit went to the Kremlin to present her credentials. She was nervous as she drove into the enormous triangular citadel about which she had read and heard so much—the historic core of Moscow, surrounded by crenelated walls built in the fifteenth century. She looked up at its many high towers and felt very small. Her letter of credence was written in Hindi with a Russian translation and was signed by George VI as Head of State for India. There were still two more days before her country would be free, when such documents would be signed by the president of an independent India.

As the Ambassador entered the vast, museum-like Grand Palace, it seemed to her that she was facing a multitude—"at least five thousand!" she said afterwards. There were hundreds of officials, reporters, cameramen, and her own staff who had accompanied her. The ceremony was extremely formal as Madame Ambassador presented the letter, asking that Vijaya Lakshmi Pandit be received as the representative of India, to the Chairman of the Presidium of the Supreme Soviet. The reply of acceptance was in Russian and, to her surprise, was followed by a perfect translation in Hindi. The formalities over, Mrs. Pandit returned to her hotel. The diplomatic career of Madame Ambassador had begun.

It was appropriate that the first social function for which Vijaya Lakshmi Pandit was responsible as an ambassador was on August 15, 1947, to celebrate India's independence. As soon as she arrived in Moscow, the Ambassador had arranged for a reception to be held in one of the hotels. It was a festive occasion attended by the diplomats of many nations who came to give their congratulations and good wishes to the Ambassador on this very important day in Indian history.

Although it was disappointing to Mrs. Pandit to be so far from home on that special occasion, it was a delight to hear her brother speak on the radio as the first prime minister of an independent India.

After World War II, Moscow, like most cities of Europe, had a great shortage of houses. Consequently, for months a long list of diplomats had waited for residences. To her surprise, the Indian Ambassador was immediately given one, said to be the finest building ever assigned to a foreign diplomat. "Mrs. Pandit," one official commented, "went straight to the head of the diplomatic queue!" It was not a large house but was finely proportioned and quite adequate for the needs of the Indian Embassy.

With her love of the artistic and her concern that a house should be homelike, Mrs. Pandit, when she entered, took one look and exclaimed, "Lekha, we can't live with this furniture!" They asked the wives of several of the diplomats what they did about household equipment and learned that they usually went to Sweden, where excellent furniture could be bought and shipped to Moscow. So very shortly *The Manchester Guardian*, which was following all the activities of the new ambassador with interest, reported to its readers that Madame Ambassador and her daughter had left for Stockholm to buy furniture and fittings for the Indian Embassy.

Lekha was a great asset to her mother. She had her father's linguistic ability and soon was speaking enough Russian to supervise the servants and do the shopping. Both Mrs. Pandit and Lekha studied Russian, read Russian history and often went to the opera or ballet, for at first official duties were not time-consuming. Most social contacts were largely with other diplomats. Mrs. Pandit soon felt quite at home in Moscow, for she found there were Russian customs that reminded her of India. Consequently, the new ambassador adapted quickly and easily to her new life.

After their return from Stockholm, the Ambassador was informed she was again to head the Indian delegation to the Second General Assembly of the United Nations, to open in September. Almost immediately, therefore, Mrs. Pandit and Lekha left for the United States and a reunion with Tara and Rita. Tara, her college work over, was to return the next month to India. She would stay in Delhi in the Prime Minister's house with her uncle and her cousin Indira, whose children, Rajiv, now three, and Sanjay, ten months old were the delight of their grandfather, Jawaharlal Nehru.

At the General Assembly, Vijaya Lakshmi Pandit was again the only woman to head a delegation, although there were a few women delegates and alternates. As soon as the session was over, she and Lekha returned to Moscow to take up the duties that the Ambassador had barely assumed before she left for the U.N. During their absence, boxes and crates from India and Sweden had arrived. Mrs. Pandit and Lekha set to work to blend the old and new together so the embassy would be more like home to them.

The Ambassador acquired a small staff of eight or ten. There were no Russians on the staff, but there was always an expert Russian translator. The chauffeurs, however, were Russian. So they might come to feel they were a team working together, the Ambassador instituted weekly staff meetings. After official business was over, tea was served, which gave the staff an opportunity to talk and get better acquainted with each other.

On the afternoon of January 30, 1948, the staff sat chatting. Someone turned on the radio for India news. Suddenly an agitated voice said, "We interrupt to announce. . . . We regret. . . ." To announce what? No one could make out. They crowded around the radio. There was a desperate note in the voice, which, in an aggravating fashion, kept breaking in, then fading out. Finally the official government announcement came, clear and distinct. The words were brief and tragic. Shortly after five o'clock, Gandhi, while on his way to evening prayers, had been shot. He had died a few minutes later.

Nan Pandit was stunned. It was unbelievable. She was desolate. She thought of her brother and what a tragedy it was for
him, for Gandhiji had been like a father to both of them, especially after the death of their own father. Her mind was blank.
India without Gandhi was impossible to imagine.

In the next hour, details came through. Gandhi had arrived a
few minutes late for vespers and apologized for keeping the group
waiting. Nan Pandit knew how punctilious he was about being
on time. As he came hurrying along, leaning on the shoulders of
his two grandnieces, his "walking sticks" as he affectionately
called them, the crowd had parted. All stood, many bowed as he
passed. Suddenly a young man pushed his way through the crowd,
bent low, and . . . a shot rang out. Then another and another.
Gandhi crumpled and fell. Those near him heard him murmur,
"He, Rama!" (Oh, God!)

Quickly, tenderly, the body was carried from the garden to
Birla House. In a few minutes, the great Mahatma Gandhi, beloved of all India, respected throughout the world, was dead. The
Ambassador felt alone, engulfed by a great loss. It was impossible
to believe that Gandhi would never again be there to turn to in
time of need.

That night in Moscow, mother and daughter listened to the
Prime Minister's broadcast to the nation. He spoke out of the
anguish of his soul, his voice clear, but the voice of one who had
reached the depths. "Friends and comrades," Jawaharlal Nehru
said, "the light has gone out of our lives and there is darkness
everywhere. I do not know how to tell you and how to say it. Our
beloved Bapu, as we called him, the Father of the Nation, is no
more."

When Vijaya Lakshmi Pandit was appointed Ambassador to
the U.S.S.R., a well-known author wrote that, with her world
point of view, she would be able to see each country, her own and
Soviet Russia, in its world setting, as well as in relation to each
other and to Asia. He commented that it was a case of "a highly

interesting person put into a highly interesting place" and that she might be able to be not only a bridge between the two countries but also "a pilot light toward understanding between East and West." Much of the time, however, while in Moscow, the Ambassador felt frustrated. There was so little that she, a woman of action, could do. On various occasions, she met the U.S.S.R. President, but she never had an opportunity to meet Stalin. Neither she nor her daughter was ever in a Russian home. She had to find her social life in the diplomatic corps.

When interviewed by *The Manchester Guardian* of England, she said that India was very new in the international field, but her country's intention was to create as many good-will missions as possible. The embassies and legations, the Ambassador felt, were such centers. She told the correspondent that when she first arrived she was well received because she was "the lady who won the brilliant victory over South Africa at the U.N.," but she had not had as many contacts with Russians as she had hoped for. She found that, although the average-educated Russian knew a good deal more about India than the same class of people in many other countries, their knowledge was largely of past Indian art and history, so the Ambassador organized an Indian art exhibit.

In conversation or interviews, the Ambassador always stressed the fact that India must have a period in which to build up its economy and develop its own foreign policy. "We have our own way of life," she said, "though we are willing to adopt certain good features whether of Russia or the West."

In addition to being Ambassador to the U.S.S.R., she was at the United Nations for at least three months out of each year— for the General Assembly in New York in 1947 and 1949 and in Paris in 1948. After the session in Paris, Madame Pandit made a quick two-week trip to India to arrange for the first wedding in the Pandit family. In January of 1949 her second daughter, Nayantara, was to marry Gautam Sahgal, a young businessman of Bombay. The wedding at Anand Bhawan over, Mrs. Pandit returned at once to Moscow to take up her duties as ambassador again.

She succeeded in establishing the Indian Embassy in the diplomatic life of Moscow. She made Hindi the language for all state communications from India to Russia as Russian was to India. The Ambassador created a deep impression on all she met and everywhere inspired confidence, so she soon became an asset to the diplomatic community. People liked her and appreciated her ability to carry on an interesting conversation. Her culture and her social graces made her a welcome guest and a charming hostess. The days in Moscow were an auspicious beginning for the diplomatic career of Madame Ambassador.

◈ 15
◈ MADAME AMBASSADOR TO THE
UNITED STATES AND TO MEXICO

In March of 1949, the Ministry of External Affairs of India announced that Ambassador Vijaya Lakshmi Pandit would leave Moscow to succeed Sir Bengal Rama Rau as Ambassador to the United States. It would be the first time that a woman had had such an assignment in Washington.

Official duties finished, farewell functions over, Mrs. Pandit left Moscow and returned to India, where in April, at the home of the Prime Minister in New Delhi, her eldest daughter, Chandralekha, was married to Ashok Mehta of the Indian Foreign Service.

On May 5, one of the largest crowds ever to greet an arriving diplomat was at the New York airport. There were United States officials, foreign diplomats, representatives of more than thirty Indian organizations, and friends. All had come to pay their respects to the new ambassador. It was in decided contrast to Mrs.

Pandit's first arrival in America, when there was no one to meet her and she had no idea where to go.

A few days later, Vijaya Lakshmi Pandit presented her credentials to President Truman at the White House and was welcomed into the diplomatic corps of Washington. She settled into her new home and took up her duties at the office. Her ambassadorial responsibilities, while much more demanding than in Moscow, seemed easier since language was no longer a barrier.

At the Ambassador's first press conference, there was an overflow crowd of correspondents. Many, accustomed to interviewing foreign diplomats, were surprised to find that Mrs. Pandit spoke flawless English and noted that she replied to their questions in short, positive sentences. Her English governess, Miss Hooper, would have been delighted with the news story that reported she spoke in a low, well-modulated voice "without a trace of accent." Another journalist wrote that she was "completely without pose, affectation, or feminine mannerisms." The press enjoyed the frankness with which Madame Pandit answered questions. Asked about her prison days, she quickly responded that if the story was to be critical of the British, she preferred not to reply. If, however, the gentleman really wanted information, she had been in prison three times. It delighted the newsmen that she always detected a "loaded question," and her quick retort usually exposed the questioner. When asked about her days in Moscow, she said that she had found "facilities" in Russia were not as great as in America and that one was "more restricted in one's movements."

After the formal press conference was over, the women journalists crowded around Madame Pandit, asking for comments from a woman's angle. She told them quite frankly that she was not a feminist but was concerned that women play their part in world affairs, for she felt the world belonged to everyone and that all must contribute to its betterment.

When she was misquoted in a press interview, it always disturbed Madame Pandit, not only because she wanted facts to be correct, but also because of her discriminating use of words. Ever since she first started to read as a very young child, she had liked the sound of words. Through the years in public office, she had trained her quick mind to select the most apt word to express her thought. Consequently, she sometimes admitted that she was irritated when a journalist substituted a less appropriate one.

Vijaya Lakshmi Pandit had been in Washington only a few weeks when a special event touched her deeply. On June 3, before a capacity audience, Howard University presented her with an honorary degree of Doctor of Laws. She had received several awards, but this was her first honorary degree. In later years she was to receive many others, but few citations meant more to her than the words of the president of Howard, Dr. Mordecai Johnson: "You were born to wealth and station but . . . when you lifted up your voice in behalf of the dependent peoples of Africa . . . you made yourself the dear Ambassador to the hearts of millions of human beings who never saw your native land, but who will henceforth love you and look toward you with hope."

Soon after Madame Pandit's arrival in Washington, requests began to pour into the embassy, asking her to speak. Hundreds of them had to be refused, but she accepted those she could. She felt that an important part of her work as ambassador was to acquaint America with her country. When she went to San Francisco, it was very different from her visit there in 1945 while the U.N. Charter Conference was being held. Then obstacles were put in her way to keep her from speaking. Now, four years later, she was the chosen representative of a free country and was met with acclaim. At a luncheon given by the League of Women Voters, the Ambassador said that a new motivating force had come into the lives of Indian women through Mahatma Gandhi. He reinterpreted India's old philosophy of nonviolence into a plan of action. This, she believed, could be understood by her audience because it was the principle taught by Christ, a man of the East. Although it was the foundation on which Christian civilization was built, she regretted that she did not feel it was the foundation of Western civilization today. The Ambassador added, "Peace will only come when we have cleansed our hearts and are willing to share."

At college and university assemblies where she often spoke, the Ambassador never failed to capture her audiences. If there were Indian students in the group, they arranged, if possible, to see her after the lecture. No matter how tired she was, no matter how long her day had been, she delighted in meeting them. Often they would sit together on the floor of a lounge, as they might do in India, and talk together in Hindi. She always emphasized the responsibility that was theirs as representatives of their country and reminded them they too were ambassadors.

In the question periods that frequently followed a lecture, Madame Pandit was often asked about Kashmir. She replied that India had agreed to the partition into two countries because failure to do so would have perpetuated foreign rule. She asked if it were not true that the United States had had border disputes that it had taken time to settle and urged her listeners to be patient and to let India and Pakistan work out their own solution. We have been condemned for what is called our "neutral" stand, she said when asked about neutrality, "as if India stood midway between right and wrong, undecided which path to take." She explained that India used the word "uncommitted," for she did not want to tie herself in advance to "the present or future policy of a particular group of nations" and added that India needed a little breathing space to find its equilibrium as a world power. The Ambassador always emphasized that "where freedom is menaced or justice threatened or where aggression takes place, we cannot be and shall not be neutral."

Wherever Madame Pandit went, she was asked to hold a news conference. Although she was the first woman ambassador in the United States, she preferred that no special emphasis be placed on this fact and declared that diplomatic posts should be assigned on the basis of qualifications and ability. She told reporters that in India women did not use femininity to promote their political progress and did not depend on dress or make-up to emphasize their feminine qualities. Because of their religious traditions, they took their political work seriously, she said, and with humility. Many, nevertheless, who watched and listened to Madame Pandit knew it was an asset to her country to have such an attractive woman as its ambassador.

Frequently in meeting the press, Madame Pandit commented on the way racial differences were played up. In such critical times, she told them, a sensational approach was wrong and to be regretted. "Humanity has a dark and difficult road to travel," she said. "On such a journey we need courage, endurance, and, above all, faith in ourselves and our friends."

Sometimes there were unusual duties to perform. One of the most unique and amusing was on April 16, 1950, when the Ambassador presented Shanti and Ashok, recently arrived from India, to the National Zoological Park. They were two baby elephants sent by her brother, the Prime Minister, as a gift from India to the Washington zoo.

In December, 1950, the Ambassador asked the United States Government to grant to India two million tons of wheat from its surplus for which India would pay one hundred and ninety million dollars. Congress kept delaying action. By the end of February, the Ambassador was desperate. "The crisis is now," she said. "The threat of famine and shadow of death lurks around the corner." Many people sent petitions to Congress and letters with contributions to her, often with only twenty-five or fifty cents but enough to let her know their concern. One woman wrote, "I feel I must do something personal for your hungry people." It was very moving and touched Madame Pandit's heart, but the need, she knew, was for tons and tons of grain.

In late February, 1951, President Truman made a special request to Congress for the food. The bill passed in June. Immediately the President signed it, and four days later a shipment of wheat left for India. On August 17, the first boatload was welcomed in Bombay. The terms of payment were liberal, the rate of interest low, but the months of delay had been tragic for India.

Often when the Ambassador spoke, she emphasized that India's debt to America was not only for wheat but also for ideas. In India's constitution were reflected many of the sentiments of the constitution of the United States, and she added, "Much of our inspiration has come from you. It is vital to our future and to yours that our thoughts, as well as our actions, shall be clear to each other."

Madame Pandit found it was not easy to make her audiences understand India's problems. She tried to describe the crushing poverty of the people and how, no matter what form of government India had, no constitution, however fine it might be, could "fill a hungry stomach or clothe a naked body." India's important task was to make an even greater effort to give its people more food, better shelter, more education, and better health. She reminded those who listened to her that "man has never been confronted by problems of such gigantic proportions before, which, if unsolved, threaten the existence of the human race itself."

Not long after Madame Pandit took up her duties in Washington, the Indian Government appointed her to serve simultaneously as Ambassador to Mexico, making her the first woman to carry two diplomatic posts. Not until February, 1951, was she able to make her first trip to Mexico City. Shortly after her arrival, accompanied by her military escort and the First Secretary, Ambassador Pandit went to the Palacio Nacional. Here the band played the Mexican national anthem. Then the head of the Presidential Guard of Honor escorted her into the Salón de Embajadores or Ambassadors' Chamber, where President Miguel Aleman in a special "audiencia solemne" received her. After credentials were presented, the Indian Ambassador and the President conversed for a time through an interpreter, as Madame Pandit did not speak Spanish. An interview with the press followed. Then the Ambassador laid a floral wreath on the Independence

Monument. Her visit to the palace ended with the band playing India's national anthem.

The Mexican public was curious about the new ambassador, both because she was the first woman diplomat to be assigned to their country and because few Mexicans had seen anyone from India. The newsmen were enthusiastic in their comments and wrote of her as "la excelentissima Señora." They were unfamiliar with the Indian costume but were impressed by her appearance and described her sari as "elegante y sencillo."

At the formal dinner given in her honor by the British Ambassador, Madame Pandit renewed her friendships with Mexican diplomats who had been delegates at the United Nations. In introducing her, her host emphasized the strong bond that existed between his government and India, for both were members of the Commonwealth of Nations.

Though language was a barrier, Madame Pandit did not feel strange in Mexico. The people at their stalls in the market places reminded her of India's bazaars. The Mexicans' love of color charmed her, and she reveled in their artistic flower arrangements. Showered with hospitality, it was difficult to leave when the official visit was over. It pleased her greatly when in October, 1960, almost ten years later, the Integral Union for Human Rights of Mexico awarded her a special medal in recognition of her "efforts toward the realization of the principles of the United Nations." The Union, established in 1959, adopted the principles of the Declaration of Human Rights and pledged to work for their realization. Seven medals were given to outstanding personalities, among them Sir Winston Churchill. Mrs. Pandit was the only woman. It meant much to her that Mexico remembered her brief time as India's ambassador there.

The news of the twenty-fifth of October, 1951, came as a disappointment to the many friends of Madame Pandit in the United States. It was announced that by the end of the year, the

Ambassador would return to India to run for election to Lok Sabha, the National Parliament.

"Why do you go?" many asked.

Madame Pandit knew it would not be easy to leave her interesting though very demanding post, but she replied, "Nothing matters so much as to be a part of one's own country. I've been gone a long time."

At the airport, a few weeks later, loaded with flowers, surrounded by friends and admirers, with the majority of the embassy staff present, the press photographers begged the Ambassador for one more shot, the newsmen for one last comment. In response, Madame Pandit assured them all that in India she would work to create more understanding of America, as she hoped she had been able to create more understanding of her own country during her days in the United States. She added that she felt India and America, in their basic approach to important problems, have much in common.

In Allahabad again, Mrs. Pandit settled into Anand Bhawan and almost immediately became involved in the political campaign. The first general election to be held under the new constitution was to take place shortly. One hundred and seventy-three million people, the largest electorate in the world, were eligible to vote. Almost five hundred representatives were to be chosen for the "House of the People," the National Parliament in Delhi. Over three thousand were to be elected to various provincial offices. Political parties sprang up like mushrooms. By election time there were fifty-nine different parties, and a large number of candidates were running as independents. All over India more than seventeen thousand men and women were busy campaigning. Mrs. Pandit was one of the Congress party candidates. Her old constituency welcomed her back, and she stood for election unopposed.

Campaigning gave Mrs. Pandit an opportunity to tell her sup-

porters of the days in the United States, Mexico, and especially
at the United Nations. She emphasized the privilege it was for
them as citizens to select their own leaders and told them that
never before in history had so many people had such an opportunity. She explained that even if they could not read, they could
vote. Each ballot had a picture on it, so it was important to remember the picture symbol of the party they wished to support.
The days were strenuous but exhilarating. When the election re-
turns were tabulated, Vijaya Lakshmi Pandit had been elected
with an unusually large vote.

Election to the House of the People made it necessary for Mrs.
Pandit to live in Delhi. She established residence at 2 York Place
for herself and Rita. She had barely settled down, however, when
she was appointed leader of the first "Good-Will Mission" to
China, composed of thirty-six nationally known people selected
to represent many shades of opinion. There were writers, artists,
educators, and leaders of all political parties. Later Mrs. Pandit
admitted that it was a most unusual experience, not because
of arguments with the Chinese but because of the differences of
opinion among the members of the mission. Mrs. Pandit, however, was most astute in keeping arguments under control during
their weeks of travel together. They were welcomed in Peking by
the Indian Ambassador, Dr. K. M. Panikkar, a well-known historian, who was a great help to the delegation for consultation.
It was a satisfaction to him that during the three weeks when the
group covered much territory and met many outstanding leaders
of the People's Republic of China, including Mao Tse-tung,
nothing was done that was not completely correct and appropriate. This, Dr. Panikkar believed, was due to the wisdom and graciousness of the head of the delegation, Mrs. Pandit.

After the mission returned from China, the government announced that the delegation to the 1952 General Assembly of the
United Nations, the first one to be held in the new U.N. building in New York City, would again be headed by Mrs. Pandit.

This seventh session opened on October 14, 1952, and after two years away from the Assembly, Mrs. Pandit was warmly welcomed on her return.

During this session, in preparation for entertaining a small group of college girls in the delegates' dining room at the United Nations, she took time the night before to make an Indian dish, which she sent from her apartment to the U.N. kitchen for the luncheon. She thought the girls would like to sample Indian food, and it was an occasion the students would never forget. It was often these little unimportant things that endeared Madame Pandit to people.

The seventh session of the General Assembly recessed the end of December to reconvene later, as it had not covered all the items on its agenda due, in part, to the long debate on Korea. Mrs. Pandit took advantage of this recess to return to India and to continue her work in Parliament. Early in 1953, however, she again left for New York to be at the United Nations when the Assembly reconvened on February 25, 1953. As before, she sat in the First Committee, the Political Committee, still concerned with the question of Korea. On April 23, the work of the Assembly completed, once more Mrs. Pandit returned to her home in Delhi. This time, in addition to her duties as a member of Parliament, there was an especially interesting event for which to plan. In early September, her youngest daughter, Rita, was to be married. Rita's fiancé, Artar Dar, was, like Lekha's husband, in the Ministry of External Affairs. As he was a Kashmiri Brahman, preparations, although more simple, were much like those of Mrs. Pandit's own wedding days over thirty years before at Anand Bhawan.

◆ 16

◆ MADAME PRESIDENT OF THE
UNITED NATIONS
GENERAL ASSEMBLY

When it was time to appoint India's representative to the 1953 General Assembly, to open September 15, the government announced that Vijaya Lakshmi Pandit would once more be the head of the delegation. This time, however, the announcement had unusual and special significance. At each Assembly session someone from a different area of the world was elected president. Paul-Henri Spaak of Belgium had been the first in 1946, followed by Aranha of Brazil, Arce of the Argentine, Evatt of Australia, and Romulo of the Philippines. Then had come Entezam of Iran, Nervo of Mexico, and Pearson of Canada. At the session about to convene it was Lester Pearson who would pass on the gavel to a new president. Everyone wondered who it would be. Many of the delegates felt that somone from Asia should be chosen, and Prince Wan of Thailand was suggested. But there were also those who believed that since India was playing an increasingly important part in world affairs and was one of the leaders in the Asia-Arab bloc, a group now exerting a growing influence in the discussions on major issues, the head of the Indian delegation would be a logical person for the 1953 presidency.

Through her years at the United Nations, the delegates had come to have great respect for Madame Pandit's intellectual capacity, her wide political experience, and her friendly spirit even toward those with whom she did not agree. She might have intense political arguments, yet she remained unruffled, calm, and poised. They knew her strength, for she had scored many victories as she debated with some of the outstanding figures, such as General Smuts of South Africa.

Her government was sure that Madame Pandit would have the

wholehearted backing of women the world over. The Commission on the Status of Women had been doing excellent work, especially in the social field, and had increased the delegates' appreciation of what women might accomplish. At first the men had been very skeptical of what a commission made up entirely of women could do, but they soon discovered it was a working commission that achieved a great deal. This helped to make the men more appreciative of women leaders. The women among the representatives of the non-government organizations (known as the NGO's) were a well-informed and active group of U.N. supporters. They would give strong backing to a woman leader. It seemed an appropriate time for the Indian Government to present Vijaya Lakshmi Pandit as a candidate for president of the Eighth General Assembly of the United Nations.

To Madame Pandit the decision was not a complete surprise. As she had watched the presidency rotate from country to country, from one side of the world to the other, she knew that if the day came that a country of the East was selected for the honor and if that country was India, she would be the logical person to be named as a candidate. Except for her two years in Washington, she had headed her country's delegation ever since Lord Wavell, then Viceroy of India, had appointed her to attend the second half of the first Assembly. These years had made her familiar with U.N. procedure, rules, and regulations and had also given Madame Pandit a wide circle of friends and acquaintances among the delegates, the Secretariat, and the press. Her name had been among those mentioned for Secretary-General after Trygve Lie resigned in November of 1952. So she was prepared, although the world was not, for the news that her country would present her for president of the Eighth General Assembly.

Rumors began to spread, and when, on September 13, Vijaya Lakshmi Pandit came down the steps of the plane that had brought her to New York, there were many reporters and cameramen waiting for her. It was exciting news for the press that probably she would be the next president of the United Nations.

Madame Pandit greeted them cordially and told them that her government had presented her as a candidate and that she understood the United States had advised the Indian Government that it would support her candidacy.

On September 15, with the election over, Lester Pearson as retiring president turned over the gavel to Madame Pandit, and she became Madame President. Many felt that the election was a unique combination of the right time, a significant setting, and an unusually able, intelligent, and charming person. Those who knew of Motilal Nehru, and of his faith in his daughter's ability, felt that she was carrying forward his hopes and his spirit that day as she took her seat on the podium of the General Assembly Hall of the United Nations.

Immediately, news dispatches and stories flashed around the world, announcing that Vijaya Lakshmi Pandit of India had been elected to this office of global significance. Newsmen wrote that the new president was "completely feminine" but that her mind "grapples seriously with affairs of state." Many emphasized the contrast between a delightful feminine appearance and manner and "a strong masculine grip on matters of moment." The *Observer* of London reported that in the days ahead the United Nations would be concerned with an attempt to reach a more settled state of affairs in the world and in this critical period had chosen for its president "the most distinguished woman in Asia today."

Cables, telegrams, and hundreds of letters poured into the office of the president, coming from cities, towns, and remote villages the world over. Many came from women. It was often evident that those who wrote were unaccustomed to expressing their thoughts to someone in a position of importance but felt they must let the new president know their hope that she might lead the world a few steps nearer to peace. Women's organizations hailed the election as the culmination of half a century of struggle for the rights of women.

It is the responsibility of the president to preside over the General or Steering Committee, made up of the vice presidents and the chairmen of the seven Assembly committees. These are concerned with political, economic, social and cultural, trusteeship, budget, and legal matters, with an ad hoc committee created to take over some of the items of the First Committee, the Political, which has more work than it can dispose of in the few months of the Assembly. Countries rather than individuals are elected to serve as vice presidents, the head of the delegation carrying the responsibility. Chairmen of committees, however, are formally nominated and elected as individuals, chosen because of their ability in a special field and with consideration for geographic distribution.

The General Committee met in 1953 the day after the opening session to consider the provisional agenda and decide which items should be recommended to the Assembly for discussion and to delegate the items to the various committees. This required careful preparation on the part of the President, for there were seventy-two items on the provisional agenda. After two hours of debate, it was decided that all of the items should be recommended to the Assembly for adoption.

The dignity and wisdom with which Madame Pandit presided won the admiration of the members of the General Committee. On one occasion when it met, and she knew the items to be discussed would involve conflicting views and intense feeling, she made a special appeal to the members to do their best to discuss the subject as calmly and objectively as possible. If a delegate forgot her admonition, he usually apologized to the President and said he would try not to let it happen again.

When presiding over the General Committee and even in the plenary sessions of the Assembly, Madame Pandit succeeded in creating, in an intangible way, an atmosphere in which it was possible for the delegates to do their work and carry on their discussions with a minimum of friction.

In the early days of the general debate, as delegates came to the speakers' dais, they turned, bowed courteously, and expressed to Madame Pandit their pleasure that she had been elected. People noted the extra courtesies and the chivalrous spirit with which the delegates treated the President. Madame Pandit wanted to be thought of and treated as a person, not as a woman. Yet she was a woman, an unusually attractive one, and the men recognized this and were very gallant to her. When Ambassador Hernan Santa Cruz of Chile presented the report of the Commission on the Racial Situation in the Union of South Africa, a subject that deeply concerned Madame Pandit, the occasion was brightened by the roses he placed on the document he handed her.

Madame Pandit enjoyed her press conferences, though she disliked stupid or obvious questions, for she was known to many as one who did not "suffer fools gladly." A story was told of her first meeting with the press after her election. An inquiring correspondent asked the color of her sari. She flashed back a question: "Did you ask my predecessor the color of his tie?" Reporters were amazed at the breadth of her international knowledge, her background of information concerning the United Nations, and the directness of her replies to their questions. When the U.N. Correspondents' Association entertained Madame Pandit at dinner, she delighted them by saying she believed there was no corps of press and radio people anywhere in the world to match theirs in zeal for news. She told them she felt they were all "comrades of the road—the road to peace." She closed her remarks to the correspondents with a stirring appeal: "You of the press have the power to sway men's minds and influence their judgments. Will you not help us to reach our common goal through love and faith rather than fear?"

As the days went by, Vijaya Lakshmi Pandit found herself thinking of the United Nations building as a home rather than an institution. She told a group of women who gathered in the General Assembly to hear her, "This Hall has begun to take on an atmosphere that we associate with a place where friends come to think and work together." She believed that, as people became accustomed to the U.N. and accepted it as an integral part of their daily lives, they would turn to it with confidence and trust. When she spoke, Madame Pandit often urged her audiences to help people realize that the United Nations was an instrument for "harmonizing dissimilar interests, reconciling forces, and channeling men's energies and genius toward cooperative action on a world-wide scale."

To her surprise Madame Pandit found that in many ways her new task was easier than being head of the Indian delegation. Then she had had to keep closely in touch with her government, be careful to reflect its views correctly on questions that concerned India, and attempt constantly to be aware of the stand other countries took or might take on matters under discussion or to be discussed. As president, her chief duty was to preside, and this she was accustomed to doing. Her years of experience at the United Nations had made her familiar with procedure, and if she needed assistance in making a ruling or settling a parliamentary point, the Executive Assistant, Dr. Andrew Cordier, was always there to advise her. "He is a tower of strength!" she told friends. Dr. Cordier, in turn, found it a pleasure to work with Madame Pandit, for he felt she handled her responsibilities well and was most conscientious in giving full attention to what was expected of her as president.

In order to increase cooperation among the members so that the work of the Assembly might be accomplished in the time allotted, she often gave small luncheons or dinners, where delegates might come to know each other better and could discuss their various points of view and exchange ideas. Some people wondered if the delegates, almost all men, would turn to her with the same freedom and frankness they had felt for her predecessors. They did; there was no difference. Madame Pandit was the President, and that was all that mattered to them.

Madame President did find it trying to sit for hour after hour, unable to move from her presidential chair. If the matter under discussion was not too important, she might ask one of the vice presidents to relieve her for a brief time. This she also did in order to give each vice president an opportunity to preside at some time during the Assembly. But most of the time she was in her place, for it demanded constant vigilance on her part—seated as she was above and behind the dais from which the delegates spoke, never able to see the face of the one who was speaking—to detect any change of emphasis, the expression of a new point of view, or a shift in the position of a delegation. She succeeded admirably, however, and during the weeks of the General Assembly session, the reputation that Madame Pandit had already established, especially for impartiality, was strengthened.

Each year, the outstanding social event at the United Nations is the reception given by the President and the Secretary-General for the delegates and their wives. In 1953 Madame Pandit was the charming and gracious hostess. It was, for Dag Hammarskjöld, the first occasion to be host, as it was not until April, 1953, that the General Assembly confirmed the nomination of Mr. Hammarskjöld. So the Eighth General Assembly was the first one where he functioned as Secretary-General.

During the session important action was taken in various areas. Technical Assistance for the Underdeveloped Nations was expanded with members invited to increase their offers of study and training to the less fortunate countries; the Good Offices Commission for South Africa and the office of the High Commissioner for Refugees were continued. What especially pleased the President was that the Children's Fund, UNICEF, organized in 1946 as an emergency fund, was made a permanent part of the United Nations.

On United Nations Day, October 24, 1953, the American Association for the United Nations arranged a most effective out-of-doors celebration, using as a setting the emergency ramp on the side of the General Assembly building, which runs along the second story like a balcony. Here the leaders of the delegations and special guests were seated, while the public sat or stood on the roadway below.

An overture, played by a band, was followed by an impressive roll call of the flags. Boy Scouts, led by an Eagle Scout, carried the flags of the member nations out of the U.N. building, up the ramp, and then placed themselves along one side to make a colorful passage, up which, preceded by two large U.N. flags, the President and the Secretary-General walked to their seats above. When the President spoke, she told the audience: "The twenty-fourth of October, 1945, marked the beginning of a great challenge . . . for we are members of the first generation of men who dared to believe that the miseries which afflict two-thirds of mankind are not inevitable." She added, "We have set out to develop and share the resources of the earth and the resources of the mind for the benefit of all." Madame Pandit's speech over, Mrs. Roosevelt presented her with a gavel in a silver box and said, "The President has lighted a lamp in our hearts, a lamp of understanding and good will." The gavel, Mrs. Roosevelt said, was given in appreciation of the part Madame Pandit had played and was playing on behalf of those whom the Charter of the United Nations called "We, the people."

November 14 was the seventh anniversary of the establishment of UNICEF and a day Madame Pandit often recalled. Seven New York City schools each sent seven children to present an enormous seven-tier birthday cake to the President. The children crowded into her office, where one of them gave a well-memorized presentation speech. Madame Pandit accepted the cake, and each child had a generous slice. Then she said to them, "I'm feeling lonely today, for it is my brother's, Prime Minister Nehru's, birthday, and I cannot celebrate it with him. I don't like to eat cake very much, so you have had to eat it for me. But what would make me happy would be if each of you would give me a kiss." Eagerly they crowded around her. When the last sticky kiss had been deposited on her cheek, one chubby youngster very solicitously asked, "Now do you feel better?"

During the 1953 session, Madame Pandit welcomed many distinguished guests who came to visit the United Nations. In October she introduced the President of Panama to the Assembly. In his speech he stated that "the age-old idea that war is a usual and normal means of settling disputes between nations has finally been rejected by civilized peoples." He expressed his belief in negotiation, mediation, arbitration, and judicial settlement of disputes.

In November, Madame President and the King of Greece, followed by the Queen of Greece and the Secretary-General, walked down the central aisle of the Assembly Hall together. Madame Pandit looked very diminutive beside the unusually tall king. "More than two thousand years ago," King Paul's speech began, "our Greek philosophers proclaimed the truth that man's spirit is free and shall not be enslaved." He closed with the hope that the United Nations might become "a cathedral where we can worship what is best in each other."

The day before the General Assembly was to close, December 8, 1953, a special session was called for 4 P.M. There was an air of excitement at the U.N. building; long lines waited in the visitors' lobby hoping for tickets, most of them in vain. People came hurrying into the auditorium to fill every seat; many stood. The regular session was suspended at three-fifty, and the President with the Secretary-General left the Hall. A few minutes passed; then the Executive Assistant, who had remained on the podium, asked that all stand.

Exactly at four o'clock, up the ceremonial ramp from the visitors' entrance to the second floor came a distinguished guest, escorted by the Secretary-General. Madame President stood waiting on the Assembly floor to receive them. Together they went through the marble-lined, tunnel-like entrance into the General Assembly Hall. As Madame President emerged, accompanied by the two men, applause broke out.

On this day, however, the eyes of the packed hall were not on the President of the General Assembly but on a man whom all knew but few from other countries had ever seen, Dwight D. Eisenhower, President of the United States.

When Mr. Eisenhower was seated in the high-backed chair on the podium, Madame President presented the delegates and the visitors to him and invited him to speak. A burst of applause again greeted President Eisenhower, who began by expressing his pleasure that this opportunity had come to him to share with them what was in his mind and heart. The atomic age, he said, had moved forward with such rapidity that he believed every citizen should have some comprehension of its global development.

An almost breathless silence pervaded the Assembly Hall as very gravely he said, "Today, the United States' stockpile of atomic weapons, which of course increases daily, exceeds by many times the total of all the bombs and all the shells that came from every plane and every theatre of war in all the years of the Second World War." But, he continued, he refused to think that "two atomic colossi were doomed malevolently to eye each other indefinitely across a trembling world." The gravity of the times, he believed, demanded that every avenue of peace should be explored, no matter how "dimly discernible" it might be, for this "greatest of destructive forces can be developed into a great boon for the benefit of mankind." Then most impressively he declared that the use of atomic energy for peaceful purposes was no idle dream of the future but a reality of the present.

Madame Pandit wished she might have seen his face as President Eisenhower closed his speech with ringing words. "The United States pledges before you, and therefore before the world, its determination to help solve the fearful atomic dilemma, to devote its entire heart and mind to finding the way by which the miraculous inventiveness of man shall not be dedicated to his death but consecrated to his life." Madame President was glad that Eisenhower's "Atoms for Peace" speech as it came to be called, was delivered during her term of office.

It was 3 P.M. on December 9. For the last time, the Eighth General Assembly was called to order. The items of business were finished. "It remains for me to thank you . . ." the President said. She was about to ask that all stand for the closing minute of silence when requests to speak came from many delegates, and there followed a most remarkable outpouring of appreciation for the work of the President. As a past president, Mr. Pearson of Canada spoke first, stating that he knew that one who presided over an Assembly of sixty nations with close to a hundred items to consider accepted a heavy responsibility. "This," he said, "you have discharged with queenly grace and unquestionable impartiality." The Belgian delegate declared that one of his most cherished memories would be the charming simplicity with which she had presided and the team spirit that the President had inspired in all of them. In his tribute the representative of Mexico declared, "You are an example of the happy combination of the simplicity of greatness and the greatness of a profound and disciplined mind." Again and again delegates came to the dais to express to the President and the Assembly what they felt. The French Ambassador with deep sincerity said, "You have never deviated from the great impartiality which from the very first won our confidence."

The delegate of Iran spoke for all the Arab countries. His comments had special significance, for he said, "When you sat in your chair for the first time, I looked to the rostrum and wondered how times have changed. Many of us could not have hoped, in our wildest dreams, that an Asian woman would one day rise to this august position. It has come to pass because you, and other women like you, have broken the shackles of centuries." The last one to speak was the head of her own Indian delegation, Krishna Menon, who said, "We are extremely grateful to you, Madame President . . . and we are very proud of you."

It was 6:10 P.M. when the President called on the delegates to stand for the closing minute of silence. Then the gavel fell. The Eighth General Assembly of the United Nations was now history.

The duties of Vijaya Lakshmi Pandit, however, were not over. Her term of office continued until September of the coming year, 1954, when the General Assembly would again meet and elect a new president to take over from her. To her surprise, invitations came from the governments of many of the member states, asking her to visit their countries in her capacity as president of the General Assembly. It was not possible to accept all, but Madame Pandit visited as many countries as she could. Among them were Ceylon, Burma and Thailand, Indonesia, Japan and Malaya, Yugoslavia, Switzerland (although not a member of the U.N.), and the United Kingdom.

In each country the President spent two or three days, longer if she could. They were days crowded with meetings and entertainments in her honor. No United Nations' president had ever before made such a tour. Madame President found it a unique experience and enjoyed it. Often she was introduced as "The First Citizen of the World." In almost all of the countries, it was the first opportunity for ordinary citizens, or even for government officials, to see face to face the president of the world organization to which their country belonged. As she told of her work in the General Assembly, the U.N. took on new significance.

It was an inspiration for the women in those countries where they had only recently begun to play a part in political life to see a woman who was so deeply concerned with politics. It was almost unbelievable that she was a woman of the East, feminine as they were, a mother as many were, a woman who had suffered for her country. It was astonishing that this lovely, gracious woman had been a minister and member of Parliament in her own country, a diplomat and ambassador to other countries, and now was Madame President of the General Assembly of the United Nations.

As she went from country to country, Madame Pandit gave

courage to many women to continue their efforts to break down age-old barriers and to find a way to make a more significant contribution in national and international affairs.

◈ 17

◈ HIGH COMMISSIONER TO THE COURT
OF ST. JAMES'S AND AMBASSADOR
TO IRELAND AND TO SPAIN

In September, 1954, Mrs. Pandit came from India to New York to fulfill her last responsibility as president of the General Assembly of the United Nations. It was the duty of the retiring president to open the next session. Her arrival at the U.N. headquarters was a triumphal entry. The delegates she had known in the past welcomed her back warmly. The creating of international friendships was to her one of the important assets of the world organization. Many times during the Assembly she, as president, had given luncheons or dinners for a few delegates in order that they might come to know each other better. Often she had seen people from different countries and of different races, as they worked together, gain respect for each other and frequently become staunch friends.

On September 21, Madame President called the ninth session of the General Assembly to order, made her farewell speech, and after the election handed the gavel to Dr. Eelco N. van Kleffens of the Netherlands, the new president. This task performed, she returned to Delhi.

With the variety of diplomatic experiences that now had been hers, it was not a surprise to anyone that on October 2, 1954, the Government of India announced Vijaya Lakshmi Pandit had been appointed High Commissioner in London. It was a distinguished post, the most important one in India's diplomatic service. She would also be the first woman ambassador to the Court of St. James's. Mrs. Pandit was pleased with the appointment. She knew and loved England and undoubtedly agreed with Samuel Johnson who said, "A man who is tired of London is tired of life."

Commenting on her appointment, *The Sunday Times* of London stated that Mrs. Pandit now had more diplomatic experience than any other woman in history. Ela Sen, in the magazine *Housewife*, wrote that there were three stars in the diplomatic firmament, Moscow, Washington, and London. Vijaya Lakshmi Pandit had gathered all of these and "pinned them to her personality as she would diamond stars in her silver grey hair."

A few days after her arrival in London, the State Landau, drawn by two horses, with driver and footman, came to India House. The High Commissioner was helped into the ornate carriage by the Marshal of the Diplomatic Corps. A crowd gathered, traffic was stopped, and people lined the streets to watch the carriage pass en route to Buckingham Palace. After it had lurched and lumbered its way there, for the landau is not a comfortable conveyance, it was driven through the great gates, across the courtyard, and stopped at the grand entrance of the palace. Here the Vice Marshal of the Diplomatic Corps and the Equerry-in-Waiting, the officer responsible for the Queen's horses, were waiting to receive the High Commissioner. As they entered the palace, the Marshal presented the Master of the Household, and together they conducted Mrs. Pandit to the Bow Room.

A few minutes after arrival, word came that the Queen was ready to receive the representative of India. With the Marshal on her right and the Master of the Household on her left, the High Commissioner was conducted into the 1844 Room into the Presence of the Queen. They entered, took one step, and bowed. They took a second step, bowed again, and paused, as in a clear, distinct voice the Marshal announced, "The High Commissioner for India." The men then withdrew, and Madame Pandit, looking very dignified and very beautiful in a black sari, went forward and bowed again. The large envelope she carried contained her letter of credence, written in Hindi with an English translation. She presented this to the Queen. Formerly these letters, written from the head of one state to the head of another, were very ornate. Now they are much simpler. It was the first time that one had been presented at the Court of St. James's that read, "We request that you will give credence to all *she* will communicate in our name."

Formalities over, Queen Elizabeth conversed informally with Mrs. Pandit and expressed her pleasure that India had chosen a woman as high commissioner. The audience ended. Formerly, a diplomat was expected to back out of the room. Now the ancient custom had been altered, and Mrs. Pandit merely bowed, turned, left the room, and went to the waiting carriage, which took her to the residence of the Indian High Commissioner, at Number 9, Kensington Palace Gardens.

This long, broad, tree-lined avenue, with high, ornate wrought-iron gates at each end, runs the entire length of Kensington Gardens from Notting Hill Gate to Kensington Road. No streets and only one footpath cross it. In prewar days, it was known as Millionaires' Row. Here wealthy Britishers, and a number of people from other countries who wished to have a London residence, built spacious mansions. Those on the side of Kensington Gardens, as Number 9 was, had rear gardens, which were separated from the park by low walls, so the occupants could look out to a wide expanse of lawn, trees, and flower gardens, where people sat or strolled, rode horseback or drilled, and where children played.

After the war, with taxes high and servants difficult to secure, many owners sold these houses to foreign governments to be used as embassies. India was fortunate to secure Number 9, built and furnished by an American woman. The Japanese Embassy was across the road, the French two doors down. The Philippines, Finland, the U.S.S.R., Lebanon, and others were located nearby. The drawing room of Number 9 was very French. It had a parquet floor, paneled walls (which the former owner had brought from a seventeenth century French château), satin upholstered furniture, and gold-framed mirrors, which reached almost from the floor to the ceiling. At first the High Commissioner despaired of changing the French atmosphere into something appropriate for an official Indian residence. Brass statues, Indian ornaments and pictures eventually created a pleasing blend of East and West. The large, unusual pictures of Gandhi, Nehru, and the Pandit daughters were a reminder to guests that this was also the home of Vijaya Lakshmi Pandit.

The drawing room was delightful for large functions, but the High Commissioner usually interviewed individuals or entertained a few friends in the small library across the hall. But it was the sitting room in Mrs. Pandit's suite on the second floor that most truly reflected her personality and interests. It was informal and friendly. Several low bookcases contained choice books, both old and new. Writers, publishers, and friends, knowing her love of reading, sent many to her, and she bought many. On her bedside table or near her favorite chair in the sitting room, there was usually a recent book, frequently an advance copy, sometimes sent with a request for comments. Mrs. Pandit's ability to read rapidly meant that usually a book was begun and finished in one evening. In front of the fireplace, on a low table, were piled the day's newspapers, both morning and evening, which she scanned regularly to keep up to date on world events. They were carefully filed for reference, as Mrs. Pandit has a most retentive memory and frequently knows the exact date she has read an article she wishes to refer to. In the same way, she knows her books and would always go quickly to the shelf to find what she wanted. She disliked having anyone replace books for her. Frequently they were put where they did not belong, which disturbed her.

Photographs of daughters, grandchildren, and intimate friends were on mantel or shelves and always the latest picture of the Prime Minister. Her desk was placed in a bay window, where she could look across the garden of the residence with its green grass and small fountain, to the broad expanse of Kensington Gardens.

Often she rose early on a Sunday morning to walk there before breakfast.

No matter where Vijaya Lakshmi Pandit was, flowers were there in abundance. Many were sent by friends or admirers; others she selected at the early-morning flower market. The vendors soon came to know the lady in the sari who always knew exactly what she wanted and who was always appreciative of their efforts to please her.

The press was eager for the High Commissioner's first news conference, and a record number of correspondents attended, as they continued to do whenever she held one. Mrs. Pandit enjoyed these contacts and found them stimulating, although, as always, she was irritated when stupid questions were asked. Photographers were usually present, and one remarked that he wondered if India knew how fortunate it was that the Nehru family had been blessed with good looks and were so photogenic. Well-known artists asked for the privilege of painting her portrait. Edward Halliday, who did a full-length one of her, was asked what he, as an artist, felt made Vijaya Lakshmi Pandit so beautiful. He replied that she had good features, lovely hair, and many other assets, but to him it was the sum total of her personality and something from within reflected in her face that gave it such rare beauty.

The duties of the High Commissioner were not very different from her former ones as ambassador, only more numerous. In addition to maintaining relations between India and the United Kingdom and contacts with ambassadors of other countries, there was a special relationship with the high commissioners of the members of the Commonwealth. In her childhood, Nan Nehru had learned about the British Empire on which "the sun never set." Then the day came when one no longer spoke of the Empire but of the British Commonwealth of Nations. Later, as more of the members became independent countries, the label British was dropped and the group was known as the Commonwealth of Nations. This the Republic of India had joined when independent.

At first, when the high commissioners gathered at 10 Downing Street for consultations with the Prime Minister or on other official occasions, it seemed odd to have a woman present, although perfectly natural to her. She realized it would take time for the men to think of her not as Madame Pandit but as the official representative of the largest country in the Commonwealth family. Quickly, however, they recognized the breadth of her international experience, accepted her, and came to value her opinions.

No sooner had the announcement of the arrival in London of Vijaya Lakshmi Pandit as India's High Commissioner been released than invitations began to pour in for both official and private functions. There were also, in ever increasing numbers, requests for her to address a meeting, participate in a discussion, receive a visiting delegation, give out prizes at a school competition, open a bazaar, be present at an art exhibit, visit a factory filling an Indian Government order, or to participate in many other often unexpected and surprising events. She accepted when she felt the cause was a worthy one and when she could fit the engagement into her busy schedule. But scores of requests the High Commissioner had to refuse. She accepted, when possible, invitations that took her to cities and towns in different parts of England, Scotland, or Wales.

It was not long before people came to feel it was a privilege to be invited to a function at the residence of the High Commissioner, for Madame Pandit was a most gracious hostess. Her invitations were accepted with pleasure and anticipation. At dinner parties, she usually sat on one side at the middle of the table in order to keep conversation going in all directions and across the table. She was not given to much "small talk" and usually led the conversation into a discussion on some subject of current interest.

When Boudhi, the cook who had been with various members of the Nehru family for almost thirty years, arrived in London, it was possible to serve guests either a European or an Indian meal, whichever Mrs. Pandit thought they would most enjoy. If Indian, the food was served on individual thalis, which made the table unusual and attractive to English guests and a delight to Indian friends. Bearers from India, Sita Ram and Josef, came to serve as butlers. They added to the Indian atmosphere of the residence. There were receptions and teas, dinners and luncheons to be given, in addition to all the official duties. Life for the High Commissioner became more and more demanding. She often wondered if ambassadors with wives appreciated their good fortune in having someone to share the load and relieve them of much of the social responsibility that was an inevitable part of diplomatic life.

In spite of the innumerable demands made upon her, one of the rare traits of Mrs. Pandit was her ability to give her guests a feeling that she was completely calm and unharassed. Behind the scenes a few minutes before their arrival, there might have been confusion and turmoil, with staff and servants dashing in every direction to do the last chores. But everyone responded to the demands that might send them scurrying up or down stairs, running to store or flower shop, searching for a lost key or a suitable vase for the flowers that had just been delivered. Yet out of all the confusion swirling around her, Vijaya Lakshmi Pandit would emerge completely unruffled, not a hair out of place, to greet her guests and enchant them with her graciousness, her tranquillity, and her poise.

The guest rooms of the spacious house made it possible to entertain visitors. The rooms were seldom empty. Officials, family, and friends arrived frequently. Mrs. Noreen Parkes, the social secretary, an attractive, competent Englishwoman, was kept busy fitting them in and adjusting the High Commissioner's schedule so that she might spend some time with her house guests, if possible at a theater, for the theater was one of the High Commissioner's special delights in London. A good play helped her to relax and forget her heavy responsibilities. She came to know many of the well-known actors and also those who played minor parts. To them Mrs. Pandit's friendship and interest in their careers was an inspiration. The flowers or a note she would often send them, when she felt they needed encouragement, meant much.

The office of the High Commissioner was in India House on Aldwych Street at the bottom of Kingsway, which had been the headquarters of the Republic of India since 1947. The high-ceilinged, oak-paneled room was furnished with a heavy brown-leather overstuffed davenport and chairs. Two stiff green leather chairs were in front of the enormous desk. It was a room that undoubtedly had been furnished for the first high commissioner, Sir William Meyer, an Englishman, rather than for a small Indian woman, who at first must have felt lost behind so huge a desk. A round table at one side of the room, where lunch or tea might be served, the blue rug on the floor, and a few pictures of ancient Indian carvings were the only furnishings that seemed appropriate for the feminine woman whose office it was—except, as always, there were flowers on the desk if she was in London.

Across the hall from the High Commissioner's office was a waiting room for those who came to see her; here small press conferences were held. The visitor's book on the table had within its pages the names of many distinguished people who came on official business or to see the unusual building and pay their respects to the High Commissioner.

From this office in India House, Mrs. Pandit carried on her official duties. Since independence, relations had expanded to such proportions that it was necessary to acquire three additional buildings in other parts of London to accommodate the staff of almost fifteen hundred. All departments of the Government of India had representatives in London, so the High Commissioner's office became an extension of the government in Delhi. Because of the long contacts over several centuries, relations between India and Great Britain were close. Also, almost all the leaders of India had had a British education and were at home in the English language, so communication was easy.

As the tin dispatch boxes came in and out of the office, with green markers for Urgent and orange for Immediate, and the red-bordered files piled up on the desk, they must have been reminders of Mrs. Pandit's first bewildering day as Minister of Health and Local Self-Government, when the red tape baffled her and the files were a mystery. After her years of experience, they now were routine.

Vijaya Lakshmi Pandit never had training in organization or administration, nor even in her youthful days the experience of routine in school or university, but from childhood she had watched her father in his law office and as he carried on the work of the Congress party. Like many who enter the political field, she learned in the school of experience. The ability to organize and to delegate may not have been her greatest asset, but her associates found that once they had gained her confidence, she left them free to carry out their responsibilities without interference. She was fully conscious of what the position of high commissioner involved. As one journalist expressed it: "Madame Pandit handles politics as deftly as she arranges her sari."

It was a new experience for Mrs. Pandit to be in a country with a large Indian community. In England there were over a hundred thousand Indians. It made January 26, Republic Day, and Gandhi's birthday, October 2, significant events. The birthday celebration always began as Gandhi would have begun it, with a prayer meeting. It differed in one respect—it was at eleven o'clock, not at sunrise. India House was always full to overflowing on these occasions. Whole families came. It was a deep satisfaction to the High Commissioner to stand under the portrait of Gandhi in the auditorium of India House and speak in Hindi. Seldom did she have an opportunity to use her own language. She loved having children there and was delighted when they clustered around her, reminding her of her own grandchildren.

In 1954, McMaster University in Hamilton, Canada, established the Whidden Lectures to honor the memory of the former chancellor and to bring scholars and distinguished personalities to the university. In 1957 Madame Pandit was invited to deliver the lectures and, while there, was presented with an honorary degree of Doctor of Laws. Later these lectures were published under the title of *The Evolution of India.*

The High Commissioner again took on the title of Madame Ambassador when, on March 1, 1955, she became the first Indian representative to Eire. In Dublin, speaking in Hindi, she told the people of Ireland that her mind was full of memories of the heroic past of their beautiful land, which had greatly influenced her generation in India. "Even though we walked different roads," she said, "to reach our goals of freedom, the courage and sacrifice of Irish leaders was an inspiration in our struggle. A new bond we now share," she added, "is the democratic way in our national lives and our desire to create a climate of peace in our world."

The President replied in Gaelic and later, at a dinner in the Ambassador's honor, said that he was conscious of the fact that one of India's most distinguished citizens had been sent from the great land of India to the small country of Ireland.

Quickly Madame Pandit responded. "Mr. President, you referred to India as a great country. But I think a country is great because of its ideas and ideals, and that is what we have in common."

Madame Pandit looked forward to her annual visit to Ireland. Usually before she went, she selected from the shelf of Irish books in her library a favorite tale and a couple of volumes of Irish poetry to read on the plane. In Dublin her hotel room was always filled with flowers, and many social functions were planned for her with true Irish hospitality, as well as trips to see shipyards, foundries, and other industries that linked the two countries through trade. She was especially pleased when it was possible for her official visit to coincide with the Irish Derby, for she had not lost her love of horses, which she had had since childhood. The Irish were delighted when she told them that, as a child, she had been moved by the hunger fast of Mac Swiney, then Dublin's mayor. She had earned her first and only gold medal in an all-India essay contest by writing about it. Official duties in Ireland

were a delight, and the Indian Ambassador found it no effort to
maintain friendly relations between her country and the land of
Eire.

Since the reign of Queen Victoria, it has been an established
custom of the Royal Family to honor certain high-ranking individuals by inviting them "to dine and sleep" at Windsor Castle at
a time when the Sovereign is in residence, usually during the Easter
season. The day came when the High Commissioner received such
an invitation from the Master of the Household. She accepted,
and on arrival between 6 and 7 P.M., as instructed, she was greeted
by a Member of the Household, who showed her to her room. After
a short time in which to relax and dress, she went down to the
Green Drawing Room, where, all the guests having assembled,
Queen Elizabeth entered to welcome them.

At eight-thirty, the Queen led the way into the dining room,
the guest of honor with her, the other guests following informally.
Dinner over, they returned to the drawing room, where, one by
one, the special guests were taken to the Queen for a leisurely
talk. This gave the High Commissioner an opportunity to discuss
British and Indian affairs and matters of personal interest as
well. About midnight, the Queen and the Duke of Edinburgh
withdrew, and the guests went to their rooms. The next morning,
breakfast was served to Madame Pandit in her room. From
the window, she could look out over the green hills and enjoy the
peace and quiet of the Berkshire countryside. Shortly after breakfast, before being taken to the London train, the visitors' book
was brought to her room for her to add her name to those of many
distinguished people who had "dined and slept" at Windsor
Castle.

Honors kept coming to the High Commissioner. The one
given on November 24, 1955, by the Queen Mother, as Chancellor of London University, was presented in the Royal Festival

Hall. Sir Ifor Evans, as Public Orator, told those present that Vijaya Lakshmi Pandit in her early youth had responded to the call "for self-sacrifice, endurance and discipline in her country's struggle for independence." After recounting the political positions and the honors that had come to Mrs. Pandit, in a lighter vein Sir Ifor said, "This world figure, this great Lady of the Commonwealth, has never lost her feminine qualities . . . her culinary skill, though it lacks academic origins . . . has all the enchanting delicacy of Kashmiri fare." Then he paid a tribute to her home life, saying, "Through her family there shines a wealth of devotion. Her love of her daughters is matched and strengthened by the admiring affection they feel for her. The indulgences her grandchildren receive or entice from her is testimony to their cunningly correct appreciation of her warm heart." Sir Ifor closed his remarks with feeling as he declared: "Her deep humanity, her understanding, her concern for others, are founded upon a simple dignity and courtesy, a composure of thought and bearing and a delight in the graceful things of life." Then the Public Orator requested the Chancellor "by the authority of the Senate to admit Vijaya Lakshmi Pandit to the degree of Doctor of Laws, honoris causa."

Graciously the Queen Mother presented the degree and placed the hood of the University of London over the shoulders of Dr. Vijaya Lakshmi Pandit. For a moment, the great crowded hall was hushed as the two women, "each a Queen in her own right" as someone described them, stood for a few seconds smiling at each other. To many, it was an unforgettable sight.

In the summer of 1958, another diplomatic appointment was added to Madame Pandit's responsibilities. She was named the first ambassador from India to Spain. It was October before she was able to go to Madrid to present her credentials. On the thirtieth of October, the trip she made from the hotel where she was staying to the Palace de Orient, to give her letter of credence to Generalissimo Franco, was an unusual one. Accompanied by Baron de las Torres, she was driven to the palace in an elegant diminutive carriage, drawn by four horses. It was the royal coach of Queen Isabel II, which the Ambassador afterwards described as "a little jewel box." The coachman was in an elaborate costume with white wig and tricornered hat decorated with ostrich feathers. The lights on the side were topped with crowns; the royal coat of arms was on the door, while inside the coach was padded and lined with satin and cut velvet, with ivory and jeweled trimmings and silken tassels. Franco's guard of honor, consisting of fifty mounted horsemen in colorful uniforms and long flowing capes, which spread out like sails as the wind caught them, escorted the royal coach. The hoofs of the black horses were painted gold; the gray ones, silver.

In the palace, the Ambassador was received by Generalissimo Franco. The credentials she presented to him were written in English with a Spanish translation. After a brief conversation with Franco, a reception followed in one of the elegant drawing rooms of the palace. It was a new experience to be linked with a government so different from that of India, yet Mrs. Pandit was much interested in Spain and found Madrid a fascinating city. She visited El Prado, the national museum, with its priceless collection of over two thousand great paintings and sculpture, including masterpieces of Titian, Rubens, Van Dyck, and other famous artists. At her press conference, the Ambassador told newsmen she hoped to be able to develop cultural contacts between Spain and India.

About a month later, Mrs. Pandit received an unusual medal. It was given to honor the memory of a young German woman, Dorothea Schlozer, daughter of a distinguished historian, who in 1787 was the first woman ever to receive a degree from a German university. When only seventeen years of age, she was given the degree of Doctorate of Philosophy by the University of Göttingen. Almost two hundred years later, the university created the Dorothea Schlozer Medal to be presented to distinguished women. Vijaya Lakshmi Pandit was chosen to be its first recipient because of "her outstanding services not only in the public life of her own country but also for her unique achievements in the international world." As Dr. Otto Weber, the rector, presented the medal, he stated that Mrs. Pandit was "one of the strongest symbols of the fundamental change in the position of women in modern society." In her speech of acceptance she replied that "in most parts of the world, men and women now walk together as equals, sharing privileges and opportunities as well as the obligations which equality imposes." Then she told them that she would like to think of herself as a symbol, for nowhere had the emancipation of women come about in as unique a manner as in India, where, thanks to Gandhi, women had not had to fight for their present status but had achieved equality and social freedom quietly and without a sex struggle. Now she said people needed to take a new course and graduate in "the art of living together."

Shortly before the visit to Göttingen, Mrs. Pandit was invited by the Austrian government to address a seminar for diplomats in Salzburg. The discussion was on "Women in Diplomacy," a subject on which she could speak from experience, so she accepted with pleasure.

The High Commissioner was continually asked to visit girls' schools and nursing institutions, and several times was called upon to open new schools in England. When, in order to "forge links of friendship with other countries," the Arnold County High School of Nottingham inaugurated a plan to name its various houses after international personalities, the High Commissioner had the pleasure of performing the opening ceremony for the Lakshmi Pandit House, over which flew the flag of India.

With the strain of work and frequent travel, it was a relief to Mrs. Pandit to be able to get away from the city for a weekend. She loved the English countryside. It was especially restful and refreshing for her to visit at the home of Countess Mountbatten. Ever since Earl Mountbatten (then Lord Louis) had served as Governor-General of India from 1947 to 1948 and had successfully brought to a close the long struggle between Britain and

India, Mrs. Pandit and her brother had been close friends of the Mountbattens. The unusual friendliness and charm of the Countess, coupled with her sincere interest in social work, made her a most congenial companion. Her sudden death on February 21, 1960, while on a mission for St. John's Ambulance Brigade in British North Borneo, was a sad loss to Mrs. Pandit. It was difficult for her when the British Broadcasting Corporation asked her to pay a tribute to the Countess. It seemed impossible to believe her friend was gone.

In her broadcast, the High Commissioner said, "At a time when the relationship between India and Britain hung by a delicate thread, when a single false step might have done injury to the future, Edmina's actions, so simple in their spontaneity, so statesmanlike in their effect, undoubtedly contributed to the easing of tensions and to the opening up of that friendship which is today such a valuable asset to both our countries." Mrs. Pandit closed her broadcast with a quotation: "A soul so fiery sweet can never die, but lives and works through all eternity."

As Vijaya Lakshmi Pandit became more and more a part of the diplomatic life of London, few people stopped to think how amazing it was that a person who had three times been sent to prison by the British Government should now be received with such acclaim by that same government and its people. Yet through all the years when Nan Pandit had been active in the struggle for Indian independence, she had never considered the British as enemies. She had too many English friends for that. It was only their government that was her opponent in the political struggle. Also, at the United Nations, Madame Pandit might disagree with a delegate of another country, but she never felt any personal animosity or bitterness toward him. They were, to her, co-workers and often friends, even if on opposite sides of a question. She frequently said, "I submit that concern should not be mistaken for bitterness"—a lesson she had learned from Gandhi.

There were people who, when they saw Madame Pandit working with the United Kingdom delegates at the United Nations and then as the High Commissioner in London, would ask, "Isn't this the Indian woman who was imprisoned by the British? How is it they are such good friends?" If they questioned her, she would reply that the past had never erected barriers between her country and the United Kingdom. The bygone days were forgotten. Today they were all involved in the same struggle for international peace and good will.

◈ 18
◈ ANOTHER ACT ENDS FOR
VIJAYA LAKSHMI PANDIT

On November 23, 1960, the members' dining room of the House of Commons was crowded. Many more wanted to come, but tickets were not available. The invitations sent out for the occasion read, "Reception in honour of Her Excellency, Mrs. Vijaya Lakshmi Pandit."

Fourteen women's associations had formed the organizing committee under the impetus of the Fawcett Society. This Society, formerly the London Society of Women's Suffrage, was founded in 1866 and is now a national society for women's service. Its present name honors Dame Millicent Fawcett, who became the leader of the constitutional, law-abiding part of the English women's suffrage movement, which began about forty years before the more publicized militant movement under Mrs. Pankhurst.

The reception brought together distinguished personalities, women who were leaders in the political, professional, and educational life of their country. Representatives of more than thirty organizations came. All were there because they were eager to pay tribute to a woman of the East who had won their admiration and who had become a symbol to them of what a woman might do for her country and the world.

Dame Irene Ward and Miss Margaret Herbison sponsored the reception. They were members of Parliament who opposed each other in the House of Commons, one a Conservative, the other a member of the Labour Party. Now they were united in their desire to express to Mrs. Pandit their appreciation of her outstanding success in the many highly important posts she had been the first woman to hold.

The gathering, in addition to paying tribute, was also saying farewell. The women were aware that the day was not far distant when Mrs. Pandit would relinquish her post as the High Commissioner from India to the Court of St. James's. No one knew exactly when, nor what was ahead for her, but all knew what a void she would leave behind. The special place she had made for herself could never be filled by anyone else.

The guests gathered around the improvised stage as Dame Irene paid a warm tribute to Mrs. Pandit, and Miss Ethel Watts, chairman of the Fawcett Society, expressed the appreciation of the organizations that were represented there. Then the guest of honor was presented. They were all Mrs. Pandit's friends who had gathered, so no formal speech was necessary. She spoke from her heart, visibly moved by the group present and the praise expressed. Through Mrs. Pandit's mind there must have gone the thought of how strange and contradictory life can be. Here she was, an honored guest in the very building where for many decades the government had taken action to prevent India—"the brightest jewel in the Imperial crown"—from being lost to the empire. In those days, in her own country, she had stormed against the members of Parliament who sat on the benches in the House of Commons in the building where she now stood to speak. In those days she had said in no uncertain terms how she felt about the British Raj and its actions.

And now . . . they were all friends. She would leave them with regret. Vijaya Lakshmi Pandit had filled many posts during her political career, but none had been so completely satisfying as this one she would soon give up. Her days in London had been a

rewarding experience. Since her childhood, she had liked and admired England and the British. She was leaving, not because she
wanted to go but because she believed in "roots" and felt she had
already been away from her own country too long. Also she would
leave for a very personal reason. She did not want to miss the
growing-up years of her eight beloved grandchildren. She felt, however, that always there would be a strong link between her and
the women who were there that afternoon. If as a result of what
she had done, there now was a little more confidence in women's
ability to help make a better world, Vijaya Lakshmi Pandit was
glad. For her part, she knew that wherever she went, whatever the
task assigned to her in the future, the memory of this gathering
would sustain and uphold her. It was her hope that in the days
ahead, she would be worthy of the faith and trust placed in her.
These things Mrs. Pandit told them as she thanked them for hon-
oring her that day.

The reception over, each guest went her own way, but many
women of the West felt a stronger and closer bond with women
of the East because Mrs. Pandit had tarried with them through
recent years. Friends and co-workers, as they had watched her
carry her heavy responsibilities, had come to feel that, as each
year passed, she had become increasingly a symbol of India and a
bridge between her country and theirs. Her work was not for herself; it was for her country and for the world. But many knew that
by being herself, she had made her greatest contribution, for even
more than an ambassador or a high commissioner, Vijaya
Lakshmi Pandit was a remarkable personality.

In early January, 1961, Mrs. Pandit left London for India in
order to be there well in advance of the visit of Queen Elizabeth.
It was to be the first royal visit since 1911, when the Queen's
grandparents, King George V and Queen Mary, had traveled almost a month by boat to visit this distant part of their empire.
Queen Elizabeth would cross land and sea by air and arrive in less
than twenty-four hours.

Elaborate preparations were being made in Delhi for the visit of the royal party. It is customary, when the British Monarch visits a country of the Commonwealth, for the High Commissioner of that country, stationed in London, to return to accompany the royal party on their tour. Consequently, Mrs. Pandit left for Delhi on January 10 and on arrival went to the home of the Prime Minister.

On January 21, the blue and silver BOAC plane *Britannia*, flying the newly designed personal flag of Queen Elizabeth, arrived at the Delhi airport. Precisely at 11 A.M. the aircraft door opened. The Queen stood in the doorway. A great burst of applause from over six thousand spectators greeted her, followed by a twenty-one-gun salute. Then Queen Elizabeth, followed by the Duke of Edinburgh, descended the steps. Waiting to welcome her were the President Dr. Rajendra Prasad, the Vice-President, the Prime Minister, the Mayor of Delhi, Mrs. Pandit, and her niece Indira Nehru Gandhi, all standing under the colorful awning arranged for protection from heat or rain.

Throngs of people, often thirty deep, lined the ceremonial route as the Queen was driven in an open car to Rashtrapati Bhavan, the home of the President, formerly the viceroy's house. It was reported to be the most orderly, disciplined welcome ever given to a distinguished visitor. People seemed conscious of the dignity of the occasion.

When the luncheon was over at Rashtrapati Bhavan, Queen Elizabeth's first official act was to drive with her party and Mrs. Pandit to Rajghat. Hundreds of people crowded around the outer area to watch as the Queen, solemnly and with great care, placed a beautiful wreath of flowers on the Gandhi Memorial to honor the man who had defied the government she represented but who had done so without bitterness, hatred, or warfare. That there might also be a living, growing tribute after the blossoms had faded, she planted a young sapling. The simple ceremony over, the party drove back to the President's home.

That afternoon a press reception was held in the Durbar Hall, or reception hall, of Rashtrapati Bhavan. Here, in colonial days, the viceroy, as the representative of the ruling monarch on such occasions, always sat on the ornate throne placed against the main wall. Now the throne was occupied by a beautiful statue of Lord Buddha with the inscription: "Wisdom resteth in the heart of him that hath understanding." The Queen stood in front of it and moved about informally, talking to many of the newsmen who were impressed by the knowledgeable questions she asked concerning the press of India.

Mrs. Pandit arranged that the Prime Minister's luncheon gave Queen Elizabeth an opportunity to sample Indian food. She selected the menu with great care, and the press noted that the Queen took "a judicious helping of the Indian dishes and enjoyed them." But what must have pleased Mrs. Pandit most was the number of times Queen Elizabeth praised the leadership of the Prime Minister. To a sister who both deeply loved and greatly admired Jawaharlal Nehru, this undoubtedly meant a great deal. On one occasion the Prime Minister told the Queen that the present friendly relations between her country and his were the result of the "stature and the teachings of Gandhi." He also remarked that the old concept of India was that of "a country of snake charmers, the rope trick, and jewelled maharajas." He admitted that these still existed, but he told Queen Elizabeth they were becoming scarce. "Rightly so," he added, "because India looks to the future."

Continually there was evidence that the Queen was visiting the largest country of the Commonwealth. Everything was on a mammoth scale. There were a hundred and twenty-five guests at the President's banquet when the fanfare of trumpets announced the Queen's arrival; there were three thousand guests at the reception given by the Commonwealth high commissioners; and half a million people attempted to watch the Mayor decorate the Queen in the traditional fashion, with a gold thread garland, at the Delhi Civic Reception.

The tour had been timed so that the royal party would conclude their visit to Delhi with the Republic Day celebration on January 26. This gave the Queen and the Duke an opportunity to witness the spectacular Beating the Retreat, a military display that probably cannot be equaled anywhere in the world. It seemed to reach a new peak of performance for the royal couple. A few minutes before five the royal party was seated at Vijay Chowk, the central square, with the President, the Prime Minister, the chiefs of the services, Mrs. Pandit, and other dignitaries. Promptly at five o'clock "To the Queen" sounded in the distance with a fanfare of trumpets. Then the massed bands appeared, a dozen or more, with the pipes in the middle, flanked on either side by the brass. They marched past the camel troops and the red-coated infantry into the square to the strains of the Indian Air Force March. Then the pipes took over and alternated with the brass, the highlight a trumpet solo played from one of the balconies of the Secretariat building in front of the royal party. After the drums had rendered "Drum Beats," the crowd was silent as "Abide With Me," the favorite hymn of Gandhi and of the Queen's grandfather, was played. Finally as the bugles sounded retreat and the bands started to march up the ramp, the great Secretariat building suddenly was illuminated with a thousand lights, which glowed and flashed like stars as darkness fell.

As Mrs. Pandit accompanied the Queen from reception to reception, dinner to dinner, exhibit to exhibit in a dozen cities scattered over India, not only were people delighted to welcome the Queen but also were glad for the opportunity to see Vijaya Lakshmi Pandit, who had brought so much honor to their country in diplomatic posts and at the United Nations. The tour also gave the High Commissioner an opportunity to greet many old friends and to view at firsthand the progress that had been made through the Five-Year Plans. Mrs. Pandit had talked much about them but being away from India had not been able to watch their development. She, as well as Queen Elizabeth, enjoyed the art, music, and dance programs arranged for the royal party. As gift after gift of special interest or of rare beauty was presented, it was a delight to note the superb craftsmanship. Often Queen Elizabeth exclaimed spontaneously, "What wonderful stories I shall have to tell my children!" Later, in commenting on the tour, Her

Majesty said that the weeks in India were among the most rewarding of her life.

The day before the Queen arrived, Mrs. Pandit spoke over All-
India Radio on "The Personality of the Queen." She told her listeners that on several occasions she had seen Queen Elizabeth in
her own private setting and had always been struck by her simplicity. "Like any woman," Mrs. Pandit said, "she is devoted to
her children. I have never forgotten the radiance in her face the
first time I met her after the birth of Prince Andrew."

In Madras, a huge birthday cake was presented, in the name of
the people of the city, at the tea at the Governor's residence. On
it was one candle and "Happy Birthday Prince Andrew." Though
far from home, because of Mrs. Pandit's foresight, the Queen was
able to celebrate her little boy's first birthday. In thoughtful ways
like this, Mrs. Pandit added to the success of the tour. She was
continually alert to all that was going on and watched for the unexpected. She told a reporter that she had had a few anxious mo-
ments in Ahmedabad when, as they drove in an open car, she saw
two boys sitting on a balcony above the driveway where the Queen
would pass. They were nonchalantly dangling their sandals from
their big toes. Mrs. Pandit held her breath until the car had
passed safely. "What would have happened," she exclaimed, "if
one of those sandals had dropped on the Queen's head! India
would have been ruined!"

Fortunately, no sandals dropped; the tour went well and proved
to be a very significant one. It was a pleasure for those with her to
share Queen Elizabeth's delight as the past, the present, and the
hopes for the future of India were unrolled like a tapestry before
her.

When she returned to London, Mrs. Pandit once more picked
up the official responsibilities that the Deputy High Commissioner, Mr. T. N. Kaul, had carried during her absence and prepared for the arrival of the Prime Minister, due shortly for the
annual Commonwealth Conference. Their days together were sad-
dened by the death of the Minister of Home Affairs, Pundit Go-

vind Ballabli Pant, a close friend of the Prime Minister and the former premier of the United Provinces, who in 1937 had appointed Vijaya Lakshmi Pandit as the Minister of Health and Local Self-Government.

On March 28, a special honor was bestowed on Mrs. Pandit when Queen Elizabeth and the Duke of Edinburgh came to dine at the residence of the Indian High Commissioner. It was a tribute to Mrs. Pandit and evidence of the success of the tour, as well as an exciting occasion for the household at 9 Kensington Palace Gardens.

On August 14, 1961, Vijaya Lakshmi Pandit went out of the great front door of 9 Kensington Palace Gardens and into the familiar official motorcar that was waiting for her. It was the last time she would do so as the High Commissioner from India to the Court of St. James's. This chapter was over. She was leaving England, which she loved and which had come to be a second home to her.

One of the last honors to be bestowed upon her was an honorary degree of Doctor of Laws from the University of Edinburgh, given on July 8. In the *Scotsman* of Edinburgh, L. M. Walsh summed up her career. "There can be no doubt about it," she wrote. "Mrs. Pandit will go down in history as one of the greatest statesmen of our time. She has taken politics out of the market place into the hearts and conscience of men and women and she has done it without abating a jot of her patience, serenity, humour and tolerance for the modern world." And she added, "With the years her great personal beauty has seemed to deepen, as though her experiences of the worst and the best of human behaviour have served only to strengthen the inner flame."

On one of her cards of New Year's greeting sent while she was high commissioner, she used an ancient quotation: "The light of a small lamp may dispel great darkness; so does understanding dispel suspicion." In many parts of the world, Vijaya Lakshmi Pandit had lighted her lamp and in so doing had helped dispel suspicion and create understanding.

◆ BIBLIOGRAPHY

Baig, Tara Ali (chief ed.). *Women of India.* Delhi: Publications Division, Government of India, 1958.

Brecher, Michael. *Nehru: A Political Biography.* London: Oxford University Press, 1959.

Buck, Pearl S. "Woman of the World," *U.N. World,* Vol. 1 (March, 1947), 24-8.

Campbell-Johnson, Alan. *Viscount Halifax.* London: Robert Hale, 1941.

————. *Mission with Mountbatten.* London: Robert Hale, 1951.

Congress Government in the United Provinces, July, 1937-October, 1939. Allahabad: Allahabad Law Journal Press.

Curie, Eve. *Journey Among Warriors.* New York: Doubleday, Doran & Co., 1943.

Eaton, Jeanette. *Gandhi: Fighter Without a Sword.* New York: William Morrow & Co., 1950.

Fischer, Louis. *The Life of Mahatma Gandhi.* New York: Harper & Bros., 1950.

Gray, Hester. *Indian Women and the West.* London: Zenith Press.

Halifax, Earl of. *Fulness of Days.* London: Wm. Collins Sons & Co., 1957.

Harrison, Irene. *Agatha Harrison.* London: George Allen and Unwin, 1956.

Hutheesing, Krishna Nehru. "Nehru and Madame Pandit," *Ladies' Home Journal,* Vol. 72 (January, 1955), 34-5.

————. *With No Regrets: An Autobiography.* London: Oxford University Press, 1946.

India News, Vol. 7-14 (1954-1961). London: India House.

Kavaka, D. F. *The Lotus Eater from Kashmir.* London: Devek Verschoyle, 1953.

Khan, Abdul Majid. *The Great Daughter of India.* Lahore: Indian Printing Works, 1946.

Khipple, R. L. *Vijaya Lakshmi Pandit: The Woman Who Swayed America.* Lahore: Lion Press, 1946.

Kimbrough, Emily. *Water, Water Everywhere.* New York: Harper & Bros., 1956.

Laird, Dorothy. *How the Queen Reigns.* Cleveland: World Publishing Co., 1959.

Lang, Iain. "Mrs. Pandit: Woman in a Man's World," *The Sunday Times* (London), No. 7214 (August 20, 1961), 19.

Legislative Assembly of the United Provinces, Records of, 1937-1939.

Lie, Trygve. *In the Cause of Peace.* N.Y.: Macmillan Co., 1954.

Moraes, Frank. *India Today.* New York: Macmillan Co., 1960.

Nanda, B. R. *Mahatma Gandhi: A Biography.* Boston: Beacon Press, 1958.

Nehru, Jawaharlal. *A Bunch of Old Letters.* Bombay: Asia Publishing House, 1958.

――――. *The Discovery of India.* New York: John Day Co., 1946.

――――. *India, Today and Tomorrow.* Calcutta: Indian Council for Cultural Relations, 1959.

――――. *Letters from a Father to His Daughter.* Allahabad: Allahabad Law Journal Press, 1930.

――――. *Mahatma Gandhi.* Calcutta: Signet Press, 1949.

――――. *Toward Freedom: The Autobiography of Jawaharlal Nehru.* New York: John Day Co., 1941.

――――. *Visit to America.* New York: John Day Co., 1950.

Nehru, Rameshwari. *Gandhi Is My Star.* Patna: Pustakbhandas, 1950.

Nehru, Shyam Kumari (ed.). *Our Cause: A Symposium by Indian Women.* Allahabad: Kitabistan, 1936.

Official Records of the Plenary Sessions of the General Assembly. United Nations, 1945-1954.

Pandit, Ranjit S. *Dominion Status and the Indian State.* Allahabad: Published by R. S. Pandit.

――――. *Ritŭsamhara or Pageant of the Seasons.* Translated from the Sanskrit. Bombay: National Information and Publication, 1947.

Pandit, Vijaya Lakshmi. "The Best Advice I Ever Had," *Reader's Digest,* Vol. 68 (January, 1956), 153-55.

———. *The Evolution of India.* London: Oxford University Press, 1958.

———. "Fearless in Pursuit of Right," *India News,* Vol. 14, No. 40 (October 7, 1961), 3.

———. "India to America," *Atlantic Monthly,* Vol. 192 (October, 1953), 107-09.

———. "Nehru of India," *Wisdom* (Beverly Hills, Calif.), Vol. 34 (June, 1960), 2.

———. *Prison Days.* Calcutta: Signet Press, 1946.

———. *Role of Women in the Modern World.* London: Ramakrishna Vedanta Centre, 1957.

———. *So I Became a Minister.* Allahabad: Kitabistan, 1939.

Panikkar, K. M. *Common Sense About India.* London: Victor Gollancz, 1960.

Prasad, Rajendra. *Autobiography.* Bombay: Asia Publishing House, 1957.

Prayag or Allahabad: A Handbook. Calcutta: The Modern Review Office, 1910.

Report of Administration of the United Provinces, 1937-1941.

"Robin Redbreast," *Time,* Vol. 50 (September 8, 1947), 27-8.

Sahgal, Nayantara. *Prison and Chocolate Cake.* London: Victor Gollancz, 1954.

Singh, Anup. *The Rising Star of India.* London: George Allen & Unwin, 1940.

Sorabji, Cornelia. *India Recalled.* London: Nisbet & Co., 1936.

Spencer, Cornelia. *Nehru of India.* N.Y.: John Day Co., 1948.

Walsh, L. M. "Her Name Will Go Down to History," *The Scotsman* (Edinburgh), No. 36873 (August 1, 1961), 8.

Woodsmall, Ruth Frances. *Women and the New East.* Washington, D. C.: The Middle East Institute, 1960.

Zinkin, Taya. *India Changes!* London: Chatto and Windus, 1958.

———. "International First Lady," *The Guardian* (Manchester, July 28, 1961), 8.

INDEX

Agra, 13, 14
Ahmedabad, 57, 63, 182
Aleman, President Miguel, 144
All India Women's Conference, 99, 100
Allahabad, 11, 14, 25, 26, 44, 57-60, 64, 66-73, 76, 77, 85, 89, 98, 100, 105, 146
Almora, 83, 102, 103
American Association for the United Nations, 155-6
Amritsar, 38, 39, 40, 61
Anand Bhawan, 25, 26, 59, 64, 65, 66, 67, 68, 69, 72, 73, 79, 86, 98, 111, 146; births at, 11, 57; changes at, 39-41, 83; description of, 15; furnishings of, 16; given to Congress party, 60; mecca of students, 44; named, 17; purchase of, 15; renamed Swaraj Bhawan, 60; second house built, 33; weddings at, 47-56, 82, 100-2, 138, 148
Aranha, Oswaldo, 149
Arce, José, 149
Attlee, Clement, 126

Bareilly, 76, 114, 115
Bengal, 42, 116
"Bhagavad Gita," 24, 103
Bhave, Acharya Vinobe, 98
Bibi Amma, 24, 25, 51, 77, 78, 95, 96
Black Bills. See Rowlatt Bills
Bombay, 34, 35, 37, 57, 64, 69, 70, 72, 81, 82, 84, 95, 101, 103, 104, 105, 111, 116, 133, 138, 143
Brahmans, 15, 148
British administration in India: Amritsar tragedy, 38-9; appoints delegates to U.N. Charter Conference, 118, 124; appoints head of U.N. delegation, 128; called Raj, 35, 81, 109, 177, 178; "crawling order," 39; declares India at war on side of the Allies, 97; headed by Viceroy, 38, 150; imprisons Congress leaders, 64, 104; outlaws Congress, 72; rejects demand for independence, 98; round-table conferences, 69, 71; Rowlatt Bills, 38. See also Great Britain

Calcutta, 14, 42, 45, 56, 57, 58, 59, 67, 79, 80, 83, 117
Cambridge University, 27, 38, 43
Chand Bagh, 98
Churchill, Winston, 103, 104, 145
Cocanada, 99
Commonwealth of Nations, 134, 145, 165, 166, 179, 180-1, 183
Congress, Indian National (Congress party): annual sessions of, 57, 58, 61, 70, 103, 104; calls on legislators to resign, 98; civil disobedience campaigns, 62, 70, 98; conditional cooperation offered British, 103; Constitution, All Parties, 58; defies British Government, 104; flag, 66, 71, 89; Gandhi becomes leader, 38, 98; goal of, 38, 70; Independence Day, celebration of, 62, 73; leaders imprisoned, 64, 104; mass arrests of members, 70, 76; Moslem League, struggle with, 127; national headquarters, 60; negotiations with cabinet mission, 127; organized, 38; outlawed, 72; pledged to social reform, 70; questions British policy, 97; Quit India resolution, 103-4; Satyagraha, official policy of, 38, 40, 62; Viceroy, relations

Naini Central Prison, 65, 66, 76, 83, 111, 114

Nehru, Ganga Dhar, 12-14

Nehru, Indira. *See* Gandhi, Indira Nehru

Nehru, Jawaharlal: birth, 14; education, 18, 27; and Gandhi, 35-6, 37, 61, 137; grandchildren of, 136; imprisoned, 64, 65, 66, 72, 76, 83, 98, 104; interest in Congress party, 38, 39, General Secretary of, 58, President of, 61, 64, 86, 137; invited to form interim government, 127; leader of youth, 43, 44, 62; marriage, 27, 28; opposes partition, 128; relations with Great Britain, 84, 180

Nehru, Kamala Kaul, 27, 28, 40, 57, 58, 63, 66, 67, 79, 83, 84, 86, 102

Nehru, Motilal: allegiance to Congress party, 39, President of, 58, 61, 64, 65; Amritsar tragedy, effect on, 12, 14, 39, 40; ancestry, 12; attitude toward British, 35, 39; friendship with Gandhi, 36, 67-8, 69; and home, Anand Bhawan, 15, 33, 39, 40, 60; illness and death, 67-9; imprisoned, 65; legal practice, 15; as nationalist leader, 58, 61, 64, 65, 66; as a person, 15, 16, 17, 26, 44, 45

Nehru, Nand Lal, 14

Nehru, Swarup Kumari. *See* Pandit, Vijaya Lakshmi

Nehru, Swarup Rani, 16-7, 48, 49-50, 51, 52, 53, 54, 56, 65, 68, 79, 82, 84; attends Congress annual meetings, 57, 58, 70; children of, 11, 14, 21; death of, 95-6; ill health of, 21, 82, 95-6; injured in demonstration, 77-8; marriage, 14; as a person,

14, 17, 19, 21-3, 64, 89; presides at Independence Day celebration, 73; visits family in prison, 65, 68, 74-6, 78

Nervo, Dr. Luis Padilla, 149

Observer, 151

Ornsholt, Anna, 87, 99, 106

Oxford University, 38, 42, 43, 46

Pakistan, 127, 142

Panchayat, 93-4

Pandit, Chandralekha, 57, 66, 70, 71, 89, 98, 104, 106, 107, 109-14, 117, 122, 126, 133, 135, 136

Pandit, Nayantara, 57, 60, 65, 71, 98-9, 103, 106, 112, 113-4, 117, 122, 126, 132, 136, 138

Pandit, Ranjit: background, 42-4; campaign for Legislative Assembly, 88-9, election to, 89, 90, resignation from, 98; courtship, 45-6; daughters, 57, 60, 70-1, 114; death, 116-7; education, 42; family life, 60, 90, 98, 101; home at Khali, 102, 116; imprisoned, 65, 67, 69-70, 80, 83, 98, 99, 101, 111, 114-5; law practice in Calcutta, 42, 59; as a person, 42, 43, 46, 59, 60, 90, 95-7, 115; wedding, 47, 48, 50-2, 54-6; writings, 43, 46, 102

Pandit, Rita, 60, 71, 98, 103, 106, 112, 114, 116, 122, 126, 148

Pandit, Sitaram, 46

Pandit, Vijaya Lakshmi: aids the famine sufferers, 116, 117; All India Women's Conference, President of, 99-100; Ambassador to Ireland, 170-1, to Mexico, 144-5, to Soviet Union, 132-9, to Spain, 172-3, to United States, 139-44; ap-